The Entangling Net

The Entangling Net

Alaska's
Commercial
Fishing Women
Tell Their
Lives

Leslie Leyland Fields

University of Illinois Press
Urbana and Chicago

1 2 3 4 5 C P 8 7 6 5 4

This book is printed on acid-free paper.

Library of Congress Cataloging-in-Publication Data

Fields, Leslie Leyland, 1957–

The entangling net : Alaska's commercial fishing women tell
their lives / Leslie Leyland Fields.

p.   cm.

Includes index.

ISBN 0-252-02220-3 (acid-free paper). — ISBN 0-252-06565-4
(pbk. : acid-free paper)

ISBN 978-0-252-02220-3 (acid-free paper). — ISBN 978-0-
252-06565-1 (pbk. : acid-free paper)

1. Women fishers—Alaska.   I. Title.

HD6073.F652U64   1997

331.4'8392'09798—dc20   96-4492

CIP

To Edith Wellington Leyland
for encouragement,
for that first Mother Goose book,
for teaching us about work

Contents

Acknowledgments

This book was written and compiled through the generosity of many people. First, thanks to all the women who willingly shared themselves, their lives to be a part of this project. Without them there would be no book. In addition to those who appear here, Jane Eiseman, Ricki Ott, Cheryl Sutton, and Nalane Johnson also gave of their time and provided valuable insights.

My best reader, critic, and cheerleader from the very start was Nora Mitchell, head of the MFA faculty at Goddard College, Vermont. Patricia Foster, teaching at the Iowa Writers' Workshop, also prodded with incisiveness and grace. Neither would let me write invisibly: for that I thank them.

Deborah Savage, Ron Grosh, Irving Warner, and Larry Hansen, all fellow writers and friends, also graciously read, listened, and occasionally argued—to my benefit.

Thanks to Wallace and Beth Fields, who kept their fax and their door always open for me.

Most, I thank my husband, Duncan, and my children Naphtali, Noah, and Isaac, who tried their best to honor my office as sanctuary, and to the newest, Elisha, who had the good sense to be born the week *after* the manuscript was completed.

Introduction

Two summers ago I started a journal again—not to record the doings of an everyday life in town but another, wholly different kind of life. Every spring I pack up our house on Kodiak Island in Alaska and move to Harvester Island, some eighty miles away. For three to four months each year I live there with my husband, Duncan, four young children, and no one else. We are the sole inhabitants. We go there to be part of a commercial salmon fishing operation that includes another island, Bear Island, and its inhabitants: grandparents, cousins, in-laws, and a handful of hired crew members.

The day I started the journal again, after a ten-year lapse, was the day I began to listen, to really listen to this life and to the lives of others. I decided to speak and write for the first time to those who know nothing of this place and this work. My journal begins here:

JULY 8, 1993, HARVESTER ISLAND, ALASKA

I am about to go out in the skiff for the late night pick. It begins at 8:00 P.M. and is done when the fish and nets are done—somewhere between 10:30 and midnight. I am strangely apprehensive. The weather is fine—gray, with mists and general damp all about, but no wind and water calm enough. This is good. But it has been almost two seasons since I have worked in the skiff. I am afraid.

When Duncan suggested it, I was nursing Isaac. "You want to go out for me so I can work on getting the running water in?" he asked. I stopped breathing for a few seconds. There was a wall in front of me, a protest that said something like—I can't. That's another way of being. I'd have to pull on my rain gear, pull the skiff in, throw my whole weight behind starting the sixty-horse outboard. I have to be strong, confident. I have to face the wind going forty miles per hour in the Pacific Ocean. How to do this? How to switch? Remove the baby from my breast, my hand from stroking his head, and instead go out and kill fish, gather the dead ones, kill the live ones? Fish aren't babies; my hands aren't sentimental, but my body is. My body is tired from being sole support of this baby with a rapacious appetite. He depends entirely on me for life and living. But I will go.

I will go out as tourist, as journalist, ready to weigh my thoughts, to look again at this occupation. Before, even in my first season sixteen years ago, I had always used my mind to escape, converse about anything, consider anything beyond what we were doing. This time I will engage, let my mind be present, after, that is, I remember the work. Remind my muscles, my back, how to lean and grab, how to pick, throw lines, do all that must be done. When this body takes over, then I will see what more can be done.

The next entry records a day's work in the skiff and the "more" I was teaching myself to see.

JULY 15, 1993, HARVESTER ISLAND
I went out with Tim Gardner. Water and fish. Lots of water, not many fish. We worked off Seven-Mile Beach again. A perfect evening, though again a little bit of chop on the way down, enough to slow the skiff from its sixty-horsepower speed down to half throttle while we pounded and sent sheets of spray veering off to both sides, a curtain of ocean that made me gasp with delight. It works best in a following sea. You have to suppress instincts and deliberately plow into the front wave, bracing yourself for the throw.

I pulled in a twenty-pound silver. Under the water it looked like a halibut, just a large white-blue mass, but as it neared I could see its shape. It was beautiful. I leaned over and scooped it in my arms since it wasn't caught well, just by the nose. It was still alive. I forgot how truly beautiful these fish are. There is something mature, grandfatherly about them—their deeper color, their heft and solidity. None of us can reconcile the price for these fish—thirty-five cents a pound—with their real value. They are worth far more than money. I do not feel regret for catching and killing them: I want to save them for a feast. This is what I will do.

As we finished for the night and headed for the tender, I looked again at the fish stacked in the boat like so much wood. I tried to feel compassion for them, but couldn't. I loved their beauty, the firmness of their bodies, the fit of their scales each to each, the lines and the iridescent coloring. They are as familiar to me as my children, and yet I have no thought of killing them, of depriving them of life. They seem born to this. I cannot humanize them or give them value beyond what is already something good—to feed so many of us, to provide us with income to live, to keep us warm, to send us to school. If justification is needed, this seems enough to me.

I kept the journal a little more than a month. It is hard to hold up anything to light for very long; the tyranny of the everyday fatigues. And my life that is lived here wants me to believe, above all, that it is ordinary, that it is like any other succession of days to be lived through quietly. My journal ends abruptly on a net-mending day, one day of many during the summer when we stand on the beach tending to nets that, end to end, would stretch over a mile in length.

AUGUST 6, 1993, BEAR ISLAND, ALASKA
Net-mending day. We all went down to Bear Island after lunch and a nap, stayed until 9:30 P.M. I jumped immedi-

ately into two big holes. They took about two hours instead of one because I miscounted one of the holes and had to do part of it over. Frustrating! There is something soothing about mending net, though. I suppose it is like a quilting bee, when women sit around leaving their fingers to their own business, while they are freed to talk. These are two separate enterprises. The fingers know their job—three times around with the needle for the knot, pull back hard, yank, put the needle through the next mesh, measure with fingers, three times around, through and through. The rhythm is there, the pattern. We know it already, how it will go, how the time at the nets will be, the holes, patches, the selvage needle asked for, the one-holers, three-holers, the frustration of hitting a really huge tie-up.

What we don't know for sure is what we will talk about. There are patterns here too, but at any time we could break those patterns. I so look forward to this time of socializing, of getting off my own island to come down here and spend the day with others. I want to talk with them about good things, about deep things—things of the spirit or the mind, maybe even of the heart. Sometimes all this happens if I stand by the right person and ask the right questions. It must come from me, though. I ask questions carefully, but under the sun, with the ocean spread around us and no walls, no reminders of other lives, we are open, all of us to this. We know each other is all we have. So we talk. About our childhood. About our jobs back "home" during the winter. About school, about a good class someone took last semester and what made it good? What makes a good teacher? About one man's upcoming wedding. We talked about the furniture business, how it compares to working on a ranch. I told the joke I just heard on the kids' Lambchops tape: "Where does a General keep his armies? Up his sleevies."

We stand there on the beach looking into each other's lives while sewing up the holes that lose us fish. This
is a quilting bee and we are the country women gossip-
ing around our handwork. But we will not give our quilt
away, nor will we auction it. We will string it in the
ocean, let the tides and currents bring us fish who will
sift through its threads. . . .

This, of course, is not the beginning of the story. If I started at the beginning, I would go back eighteen years to the day I landed a hip-booted
foot onto the gravel beach of a small island in Alaska. My boots, heavy as
a fire fighter's, stood me next to my new husband, who had gained not only
a wife but a new fishing partner as well. We stood together like twins those
early days, looking alike in what was the commercial fisherman's uniform
then—black hip boots, jeans, wool halibut jackets, white pagook hats.
There's much about those days I want to forget. The adjustments of marriage were the usual challenge, but we added to the mix a working relationship, as we labored side by side in small skiffs for twelve to sixteen
hours a day in seas and winds that shuddered even the big boats, catching
more salmon than anyone knew what to do with. Those first five years
would be lost to me entirely in the blur of exhaustion, except that I kept
journals for parts of those summers, journals that reveal my own journey
from idealism to reality.

Some realities I already knew. Even before I stepped onto the beach I had
been taught, at least in theory, something about the two main kinds of
salmon fishing around Kodiak Island—set gillnetting and seining. Duncan and his family were set gillnetters, or setnetters for short. It was entirely different than anything I had seen on television or in the movies.
Rather than prowling the seas in search of salmon on a vessel large enough
to live on, as the seiners do, they were based on shore. The nets themselves
were stationary, attached to shore with a nylon line as thick as my wrist.
As the fish were caught in the nets, the setnetters would go in small open
skiffs and "pick" them out, one by one by a hundred, by four hundred, by
however many hadn't seen the web and had tried to swim through. That
single cord binding each net to shore was the best news to me: it meant a
bridge between the world of water and land; it meant that unlike the sein-

ers, we could come ashore to eat and sleep in cabins; it linked a world I knew at least in part to a world I didn't know at all.

But even that world I thought I knew was challenged. Duncan's family had fished here for almost twenty years. The system was already in place—not just the system for commercial fishing but also the system for living together on this speck of land, a forty-acre, treeless, wind-scoured island on the edge of the Shelikof Strait. We shared the island, the main cabin, and most meals with his parents, his younger brother, and his older brother and wife and baby. I learned about hauling the well water in buckets; how to reuse the dishwater to save our shoulders another trip; how to wash clothes with an ancient wringer washer; that you leave the clothes out on the line through the days of rain; that you take off your boots before entering the shared cabin; that you leave the outhouse door open to signal it is occupied . . .

I also learned about fear. After lunch one day Duncan remembered seeing a buoy and fathoms of good line washed up on some rocks on the other side of our island. It was a rare sunny day. We hadn't picked many fish that morning—it seemed a good excuse for our own little skiff trip. There was one problem, though. A huge swell from the northeast, leftovers from a storm the day before, alternately surged and sucked at the very site of our buoy rescue. I had no idea how we were to perform this feat: the swells looked impossible to me. But not to Duncan. Then came the plan. I was to run the skiff, ease the bow up to a shelflike rock, hold the skiff just close enough and steady enough in the swells for him to leap off onto the rock. I would then reverse furiously out into calmer waters, circling until he retrieved the buoy and line, then again ease back and pick him up. The plan didn't sound good even in theory. I had little experience running the engine, let alone next to rocks with the added complication of six-foot waves whose main goal was to smash the nearest floating object against the nearest solid object. But it happened too fast to even protest. Amazingly, it went as planned, lubricated with and facilitated by yelling and arm waving and high anxiety and erosion of stomach lining—mine. That was one of a multitude of "firsts" that came too fast with too little preparation.

I learned, too, about silences. The first year, somewhere in the middle of the season, Duncan and I pulled our skiff up to the tender, the larger boat that receives our fish and delivers it to the cannery. It had been a good morning's work; our skiff was loaded with pink and sockeye salmon. Af-

ter we had pitched and weighed the fish and delivered them onto the tender, Duncan hopped aboard the larger boat to sign the delivery slip. My job was to remain with the skiff, clean out the kelp, and bail out the sludge of fish blood and gurry. Finally done, I sat on the seat in the stern, feet up, ready to grab a few moments of rest when the skipper of the tender came out. He leaned over the rail and in a picture of studied nonchalance asked, "So, where did you get all those fish? From that net over there?" He pointed casually past our island to a net that had indeed been plugged that morning. I laughed to myself and remembered in a flash what it was like to be a freshman the first day in high school, to be the new kid in the neighborhood. "Oh, we got a few here, a few there," I said equally nonchalantly, waving my hand vaguely to encompass the panorama of ocean. He laughed heartily, shook his head, and went back in the cabin. I knew I had passed. Duncan had never told me outright, but I understood instinctively one of the cardinal rules of fishing—you never tell where you get your fish. Because I was young I learned and adjusted quickly to the rules, even to the grind of work that left my body aching and, by the end of those summers, ten pounds heavier with muscle and the sheer gravity of fatigue.

But you see, I am doing it, going back to the beginning. I drift back continually to the crucible of those first years because they changed me. Without them, I would perhaps be a journalist asking questions to understand women in fishing as some kind of social phenomenon—"Why do women work in the most dangerous occupation in the nation?" Or I would be a feminist academician exploring gender issues—"Why do many women who fish resist the new politically and gender correct term 'fishers,' calling themselves 'fishermen' instead?"

Indeed, this is how I started. It was much more comfortable to tackle this objectively as a research project. That I would write something about women in fishing in Alaska was already inevitable. There were so many tantalizing fingers to the subject, so many implosions of stereotypes, so many pleasing complexities and conundrums to the thing. It screamed to be picked up, turned over, and looked at from all angles. My first wonder was why—Why do women go to sea, choosing to live with three men in a space often little bigger than a closet? Why do they risk their lives, their health in this occupation? Why do some leave children and spouses behind, sacrificing the stability of the ground beneath, the certainty of friendships and home? And not least, Was anyone's story like mine? Where I live and fish, women do not talk much about their fishing lives. It is private, part of the secrecy we all cloak around the subject. Silence begins with numbers—how many fish we caught, how many red salmon, how many pink salmon, where we caught them, how this year compares to last year . . . Every family, every fishing operation holds this information tight to their chests. Secrecy begins here and grows, expanding to other areas until silence is habitual.

After a few interviews, I began to see what some of the answers were, yet every woman had a different story. As the transcripts piled up on my desk, one after another, I grew increasingly convinced that these women were worth listening to. But I had no desire to join them. I adamantly resisted inclusion of my own story, wanting only to be the conduit, the channel through which others could speak. It could have worked. The stories here are powerful enough to stand with little support from anyone else. I wasn't sure that I had a story to tell. Other women did not feel that way. Not one ever responded to my initial inquiry with an "Aw shucks, why do you want to talk to me?" Each knew she had a story worth telling, and each knew she was capable of telling it. I was drawn to their confidence but intimidated as well. I had a whole host of reasons for drawing back. Because I have come to fishing through marriage, because fishing is not my first occupational choice, because I have focused more on my four young children these last few years, because I am only involved during the summer months—for all these reasons I knew myself to be in a different orbit than these women who unflinchingly called themselves "fishermen."

But finally I was drawn in through the journal kept sporadically that begins this introduction. I had all but forgotten it, having already dismissed it as inconsequential. Later that fall, while preparing for a poetry reading, I found it again on an obscure disk and decided in a wild moment to ditch my usual repertoire and read excerpts from the journal, however raw, instead. The response to my reading startled me. For the first time I realized that perhaps I did have a story to tell and that the story could reach people regardless of geography or occupation. From that day I began to see a way into my subject—through my own story. I realized afresh the notion that the universal is sometimes best seen through the personal. And it was all there in my own life: the same issues, struggles, gains, and losses echoed by so many others, yet distinct as well. Family issues—how to nurture relationships with an occupation that often separates families for weeks and months at a time, how to work incessantly with spouses and partners and stay married. And the physical demands of the work itself on top of enduring sexual harassment and discrimination and more. The themes are similar but the particulars vary dramatically.

The question that kept driving me was, Why, out of all the occupations and professions, choose such an extreme one? I know the reasons for my choice: I married the occupation—nets, cork line, skiffs, the whole ball of web. Choosing to marry was choosing to be involved in fishing; it was that clear. For those who entered the fisheries independently, apart from relationships, the motivations usually had something to do with freedom, both economic and otherwise—controlling your own life, making your own decisions. And yet here is the twist, one of those wondrous complexities: to harness your life and occupation to earth and ocean brings a far greater dependence and helplessness. Every woman here, every fisherman, has multiple stories to tell of howling winds and tall seas breaking over her small craft, sending boat and crew desperately hobbling to shelter, an island, a cove, any kind of stay against the immeasurable forces of wind and sea. Who is really in control?

And what kind of freedom is this? The freedom to fish is not freedom from rules or laws; indeed, all levels of government circumscribe whole sets of rules around us, like a seine net encircling a school of herring. To fish does not remove all barriers, it only removes "society's," if we can use such an amorphous word. There is freedom from traditional society's expectations, but in their place comes an incredible bond, even bondage, to another set of rules equally confining. These are not only the rules that tell who, when, where, how long, how much, and in what manner fisherman can fish but also the rules each person devises simply to stay alive. And woe to those who break them.

One of the most intriguing tentacles of this story is the mythology of Alaska itself. Alaska is still wilderness, frontier—traditional male terrain overlaid with an overwhelming "mythology of maleness," of conquest, exploration, domination. Add commercial fishing and you add another layer of maleness: leadership, stoicism, instinctive knowledge of the fish and sea. Enter women. Not only women in Alaska, the frontier, but women in fishing. Not only women on deck stacking the web but women skippers yelling out orders from the wheelhouse—the world is upside down.

Tradition is on its head. If I could choose one word that begins to explain some of this it is there in Alaska's state motto: Alaska: The Last Frontier. Do you hear it? The last frontier, like the Last Chance Saloon before miles of desert. There is urgency here that supersedes gender. This is the last place where man or woman can make his or her own life, where society is loose, open, like gauze, where the rules are not yet made. The Alaska myth says anyone can come here, that this is the place where ability, courage, determination, and strength bag the biggest bear, catch the most fish, win the day—all twenty-two summer sunlit hours of it.

But, like all myths, actually living the Alaska myth is something else again. There are stories here of harassment and discrimination, of women who could work with equal ability beside their male co-workers but who were ridiculed, humiliated, or very nearly killed. No one will be surprised to read these accounts. These are old stories. What's new is that they are coming from a society so young, that feels still so wild and unmade; already we are remaking it in our same old image. But to tell it straight, these things don't happen to everyone, or perhaps even most everyone. All we can say with any accuracy is that they do happen. Listen to those stories and learn what you will.

To make sense of this book you need to know certain things. Some of the information needed is simply factual: Where is Kodiak Island? What is a "kicker"? What does a "tender" do? Much of this information appears within the text to prevent the disruption of flipping to a distant glossary. Other clarifications and backgrounds I will try to supply in the introduction of each chapter. I will forego many of the technicalities of the fisheries themselves, mostly out of necessity but also by design, for this reason. There are five different fisheries represented here: salmon, king crab, halibut, cod, and pollock. Even within a single fishery, particularly salmon, there are a number of different methodologies, or gear types, as we call them: set gillnetting, beach seining, purse seining, drift gillnetting, trolling. All of these are here as well. And each fishery and gear type comes complete with its own science, history, technology, and language. Rather than serve that subject poorly, and thoroughly confuse the reader along the way, I have chosen not to serve it at all except to illustrate and describe a few general aspects of fishing. My subject is instead people, lives, voices. Let the reader look beyond the technicalities of commercial fishing, or their absence, to the larger experience being told.

Other things you need to know: How did I choose these women? What kind of selection process did I use? How did their words arrive on these pages in this form? First, selection. No one knows how many women work as commercial fishermen, but an unofficial estimate is somewhere around 5 percent of the fishing fleet. On Kodiak alone that would mean well over a hundred, more women just in my own community than I could possibly track down and interview, not to mention those in other fishing communities in Alaska. I had to make continual choices. Since I live and fish on Kodiak Island, and since Kodiak is the second largest fishing port in Alaska and in the top three nationwide, it seemed a natural choice to begin here. I traveled to other fishing communities as well—Cordova, Juneau, Valdez—and tracked interviewees down in various other places. My goal was to listen to a range of voices spanning the various fisheries and the various geographies of this vast state. This book is not exhaustive, however, even in its representation. To limit the scope for both reader and writer, I chose to focus on ocean fishing. The stories here travel us well over a thousand miles from the Bering Sea to Prince William Sound to the Gulf of Alaska to the westernmost waters of the Aleutian chain. The book does not take us to the interior of Alaska, however, to the broad, quiet rivers where entirely different kinds of fisheries take place. Either I serendipitously made a succession of excellent choices or fishing women are inherently articulate, energetic, passionate, and honest. After more than twenty-five dynamic interviews, I know it to be the latter. This also means there are hundreds of equally exciting, insightful stories missed.

I began with taped interviews that ranged from two to four hours in length. I would personally transcribe the tapes, then put the transcript in some kind of order. Editing has consisted primarily of deleting or moving text around for clearer organization and fluidity.

While at a writing conference recently I asked a friend who was a writer in the Midwest to read the manuscript. He handed it back to me one evening shaking his head, clearly troubled. Finally he came out with it. "I just don't believe fishing women talk like this. It doesn't ring true." He stopped just short of saying that they were too articulate and intelligent. It didn't occur to me to be angry at his response; rather, I was stunned and baffled. I realized, belatedly, that as people found out about my project, they immediately shifted whole sets of stereotypes onto these women: stereotypes about the working class, about women in alternative occupations, about women who live in Alaska. His comment was not so much insult as ignorance, I decided. How could I begin to explain Kodiak to him, or Alaska? A mechanic could have a master's degree in history; there are more women than men in the firefighter's training course; the mayor is a woman who can regularly be seen in hip boots reeling in a silver salmon; after their interviews for this book, one commercial fishing woman took off for Nepal, two others for Mexico, another for Chile.

At some point, though, all answers, all implosions of stereotypes, all attempts to analyze and distill the experiences of commercial fishing down to precise definitions fail. And that is good; otherwise there would be no story. This isn't just about facts and objective information—this is about fishing women's lives and their telling of them.

Let me end this introduction the only fitting way—with a part of a story. Martha Sutro, a successful high school English teacher in Vermont, resigned her position to winter fish in the Bering Sea. Listen and you will hear why:

I remember suddenly we got out on deck and it was night when we started, or else we were working and night fell and I didn't see night fall. I just remember looking up a couple of times. You know these massive sodium lights that are shining on you so you can't see into the wheelhouse and you can't see anywhere outside the sodium lights. It's like you're in space. It must be like space. It's the only thing I can think of. But I remember looking up at one point and seeing the wheelhouse and seeing this tremendous roller as high as the wheelhouse and the sodium lights were shining on the foam of the roller. It was just enormous! It's so big, much bigger than this boat! And nothing was crashing, you're just rolling. You'd see the boat go up, take the roller, then go down. And you're on this tiny deck; you're very low on a crab boat. I just felt so minute. That was one of the most powerful sensations I could ever have in my life. I didn't feel a fear like I'm going to die here, but I felt I could so easily die, that I could so easily be extinguished and there would be nothing to account for it all.

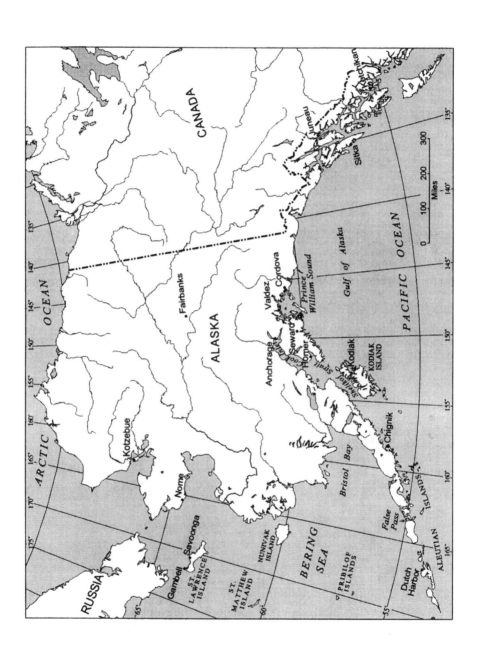

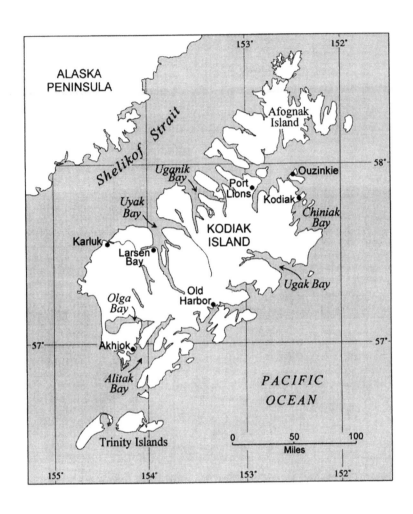

ALASKA
PENINSULA

Shelikof Strait

153°   152°

Afognak
Island

*Uganik
Bay*

58°

Ouzinkie

Port
Lions

Kodiak

*Uyak
Bay*

*Chiniak
Bay*

Karluk

KODIAK
ISLAND

Larsen
Bay

Ugak Bay

Old
Harbor

*Olga
Bay*

57°   57°

Akhiok

*Alitak
Bay*

*PACIFIC
OCEAN*

0   50   100

Miles

Trinity Islands

155°   154°   153°   152°

Virginia Adams. (Photo by Andy Hall)

Sylvia Lange. (Photo by Marchelle Espe)

Cinda Gilmer. (Photo by Tyler Gilmer)

Holly Berry. (Photo by Andy Hall)

Theresa Peterson. (Photo by Andy Hall)

Leslie Smith. (Photo by Andy Hall)

Martha Sutro. (Photo by Jeff Steele)

Laurie Jolly. (Photo by Brian Orlov)

Rebecque Raigoza. (Photo by Brian Orlov)

Lisa Jakubowski.

Christine Holmes. (Photo by Leslie Leyland Fields)

Laurie Knapp. (Photo by Andy Hall)

Mary Jacobs. (Photo by Andy Hall)

Debra Nielsen. (Photo by William Nietupski)

Peggy Smith. (Photo by Marion Stirrup)

Sandy Earle. (Photo by Daniel Earle)

Lori Francisco Johanson. (Photo by Leon Francisco)

Terri Francisco Barber. (Photo by Leon Francisco)

Leslie Leyland Fields. (Photo by Leola Harkins)

Theresa Peterson walks the docks. (Photo by Andy Hall)

Deckwork (Lorne Murphy works on Mary Jacobs's purse seiner). (Photo by Andy Hall)

Beach seining (Rebecque Raigoza works with Don Dumm and crew). (Photo by Leslie Leyland Fields)

Set gillnetting and skiff work (Terri Francisco Barber and Lori Francisco Johanson). (Photo by Leon Francisco)

Gear (Theresa Peterson). (Photo by Andy Hall)

Holly Berry with the crab pots she built. (Photo by Andy Hall)

What it's like (sometimes) to fish in Alaska (Terri Francisco
Barber). (Photo by Leon Francisco)

1 "And Then I Got a Job on a Boat"

MAY 26, 1978, BEAR ISLAND (OFF KODIAK ISLAND), ALASKA

Bear Island looks so small and lonely, so desolate. It is hard to believe this will be my summer home (and sometimes winter?) for the rest of my life. There are no trees. But there are mountains all around and ocean and sky—more sky than I've lived under up till now. And the colors, the blues and greens. The hues are so intense they almost burn into my brain. Every night this week I have had technicolor dreams, as if I'm seeing through a special set of glasses.

JULY 26, 1978, BEAR ISLAND, ALASKA

I am exhausted. At this point, I couldn't care less about the fish; I'm just trying to survive. Sometimes I wonder why I'm doing this, yet I wonder only for a minute. It's not as though I have a choice. There are only five of us fishing all these nets, twelve to be exact. It's crazy. No one around Kodiak has so many nets with so few people to work them. But I can't back out now. We're so completely reliant on one another. We can't even be sick. The honeymoon is over (was there a honeymoon?).

M y first question in the interviews was always "How did you get into fishing?" I knew my own experience, the outsider swinging in on the hinge of a ring, a wedding ring, was only one way in. And though it is inarguably both the easiest and the hardest way in, it was also the least interesting to me. I simply entered, was even invited to, a world already created, already revolving with its own laws of gravity and physics. My job was simply to learn the laws. There was a certain security there in learning under the eyes of family instead of learning as an outsider hired on as crew, but in truth the roles got all mixed up. When fishing with my father-in-law, was I daughter-in-law or crew? As he became older and as I gained experience running the skiff, I began to take over some of his jobs. Was I then skipper and he crew or were we still family? And working with my husband was much more complicated and the repercussions much more serious. Were we husband and wife on shore but skipper and crew on the water? If we were still husband and wife on the water, how then could we work together allowing for equal decision-making when one was clearly more knowledgeable than the other? Moving from dock to deck through marriage had its advantages, but it clearly had its drawbacks as well.

This story I knew. I wanted to know how other women entered into fishing because commercial fishing in Alaska is not like other jobs. For one thing, it is tightly controlled by the government. Unless you're born into fishing, or related to someone who fishes, it is tough to get in. You don't fill out an application; you don't turn in a resume and wait for the call to interview; instead you hope for mercy, for luck, for connections. Then you work, doing any job you can, hoping someone will notice you. When not working, you "walk the docks," the nautical equivalent of knocking door to door: you go boat to boat in the harbor, looking for the skipper, asking if there is any opening, for a deckhand or a cook. Usually the answer is no. To hear that, you often must endure the jeers and humiliations of the male crew members, who delight in your discomfort. But you do it; you do anything you can and maybe, just maybe, you will be one of the lucky ones who, out of hundreds and thousands who flock to Alaska for a fishing job, actually get a job on a boat. That's one scenario.

The next question has to be Why? Out of everything else these women were capable of doing, why did they choose something so dangerous, so *unpredictable, so—alternative? If not for love, then for what? Money? Excitement? Danger? Competition? Independence?*

In this chapter, there are five stories that begin to tell some of the hows and the whys, each a little differently. Sylvia Lange's story is the least typical. She is one of a comparatively few women born into a fishing family who continues to be involved forty-some years later. The other four came up from "Outside" (what Alaskans call the rest of the country), lured by various kinds of bait. If there is a "typical" story, it is somewhere in the threads that twine among the words of these more-than-ordinary women who made that first step from dock to deck.

Virginia Adams

Virginia remembers every detail of first setting foot on a working deck. It was back East, in Montauk, New York, and it changed her life. From that day she became an ardent fisherman, sometimes working with her husband, Jonathan Edwards, sometimes hiring on as crew on other boats. After seven years, feeling increasingly restricted by regulations, they came to Kodiak. Virginia found starting over, breaking into a new fleet, overwhelming at times.

That first day when I went fishing with Jon it was almost like a religious experience with me. That's how I got into fishing. I was eighteen and I fiddled around with a few things out of high school. I decided I didn't want to go to college. Jon and I had known each other all our lives. We were at a wedding and I just kind of turned and looked around. Jon caught my eye, we caught each other's eyes, and that was it. My mother said she saw me look at him and she just shook her head and went, "Oh no, that poor guy, he's had it!" So we got together. I was working in the hospital as a nurse's aide; he was a commercial fisherman running a dragger out of Montauk, New York. Jon's been commercial fishing all his life, and his father—every man in his family going back to the Mayflower.

So he said, "Come out fishing." I said, "Great!" It was spring, the decks were icy. We took off. Jon had cowboy boots on, walking around on this icy deck. He was setting a trawl [conical net dragged near the sea bottom], standing up on the rail hitting something with a hammer, and it was kind of rough. I was having to hold on and there he was. I thought—this is something! And then we fished that day. As the day went on it got calm and sunny. I was sitting on the back deck and it just hit me, you know, I was going to chuck it all, this was what I was going to do.

It wasn't just that I had fallen in love with this guy, although that certainly was part of this great feeling, but I just had this light go on in my head inside me and I knew I wanted to fish and that was it. I gave notice, started fishing, and never stopped.

So Jon's seiner had a woman hired and something happened with her right before the season was to begin. The skipper said, "I'll give you a shot, for half share—6 percent." I realized unless I got started somewhere, I couldn't argue with that. I took the job.

When I got started seining, I knew I had to do really well, and this particular other crewman would only call me "Greenie." He called me this for the first couple of days and finally I just said, "Listen, shut up. My name's Virginia, I'm not a greenhorn." We hadn't really started fishing yet, we were on strike.

Then finally when the strike was settled, we headed out and we went down to Karluk. Five of us seiners decided to fish together and split the money: they had to get the fish out of the area. We were all going to help in the chores, blah, blah, blah. Well, this one boat tore up its seine really bad. I hopped over before anyone else because I knew it was a golden opportunity and I started zipping away mending the seine. That guy stopped calling me Greenie. That was it. He never called me that again.

It was pretty unusual for a woman to be on deck then, especially one woman on deck on a small seiner with three other guys with no head [toilet]. There was one crewman, Jon and myself, and the captain. The crewman was a local boy, very popular, so whenever the opportunity arose when we were at anchor, he would hop in the skiff and go visit the other boats. The guys on the other boats were always asking about me—"Who the heck is that?" And he and I had a kind of testy relationship at first, but we ended up really liking each other and being really good friends and he's only said really positive things about me, which came back to me and made me feel good.

But you know some of that is because I stayed quiet and tried to build a relationship with him instead. I tried to let time tell the real story instead of screaming, "Listen, I can do this and this . . ." I just figured sooner or later he was going to know. There was a lot of trouble getting established, who was to do what job. But he started giving me some really good press among the fleet. I could see it coming back. People were courteous with me. They had been told I was a no-nonsense fishermen, I had skills, I was a hard worker, so I felt that fairly quickly my rep was being set in the right direction.

Sylvia Lange

Sylvia has lived in Cordova all her life. I interviewed her in the office of the cannery she and her husband had just purchased. With one month left to be on line for buying and processing salmon, she was working long hours, despite being eight months pregnant with her third child and in her early forties. Born into a native fishing family, Sylvia has fished since childhood.

I had my first boat in '67. Fishing was a family thing. That's what my mom and dad did. We gillnetted in spring, then seined, then gillnetted again. All on the same boat at that time. It was a small boat, thirty-four footer, combination rig. And we lived on the boat all summer long, the four of us, my sister and me and Mom and Dad. When I was fourteen I was given my own skiff. I didn't have state-of-the-art equipment by any means. I had what my dad handed down to me—a flat skiff with an outboard on it and a reel that ran off a small gas-powered engine. I'd fish off the boat in that skiff. So would my mom and dad. They each had their own skiffs. And then my sister would fish with my mom.

My dad provided me with nets and the equipment, and the money I made was my school clothes allowance. So a fish would come over and I referred to fish as dresses. I'd catch so many "dresses" per day. I was only allowed a certain area to fish and a certain stage of the tide. They kept a close eye on me. I still can't believe they let me do it, but they did. People didn't know quite what to think of me then. I was Fred Lange's son.

When I was fourteen, I had my first experience being petrified. It had been storming. My dad had taken the boat up to the slough to a protected area. My mother and I kept our skiffs tied up behind and stayed on the boat. Dad would go out and fish and come back. And then the weather came down, so I talked Mom into letting me go back out. So I took off and went and fished, and then when I was done I went and delivered at the tender. We didn't have radios yet. I told the fellow at the tender to tell my mom I was heading back up the slough. Well, the weather came up. I got kind of disoriented on the way up and kept running into sandbars. It was storming so hard the waves were coming into my open skiff. I had to bail while I was driving. At that point I'm crying. I remember singing "Jesus Loves Me." I don't know where that came from; I wasn't raised in a religious fashion, but I started singing something just to calm me. Finally I found the channel and got my skiff bailed out. I eventually made it back up the slough. I didn't tell Mom, of course, that anything was wrong; I said everything was fine, no problems. I never told her about it, not till many years later. I didn't want her to not let me go fishing. I had talked her into letting me go, because I could handle it.

When I was eighteen I got a skiff with a cabin on it from my dad so I could go out by myself. From the time I was eighteen on I operated independently. Nobody feels totally confident all the time though, because it's dangerous to fish here. It's a bar line [line of sandbars]. There's the Copper River Delta, and it spreads out over about a sixty-mile area on the Gulf of Alaska. There are five different bar entrances, so if you're inside the bar, you're fishing that tributary, essentially. If you're outside the bar you're on the Gulf of Alaska. It's real shallow, so it's a constant breaker line. So depending on the quality of your equipment, your boat, how many fish you have on board, what the weather's doing, what the tide's doing, it can be extremely treacherous, or it can be just too easy and boring. It's sort of the saying "You're either bored to death or scared to death." It's an area that takes some local knowledge, takes a while to get used to.

From when I was eighteen to about twenty-three, I fished in the summer for college money. I went to school in the winter. When I was twenty-three, I had my first decent boat built. I decided what I wanted and had them build it for me. I had a good year to pay for it. And after that

I fished more competitively and fished all over the area. I think from then on I considered myself more a fisherman. Up till then I sort of played with it, felt about myself the way I was treated, which was as an anomaly.

There were some older women fishing and my mother fished. There were wives of fishermen who fished. But the fishery changed so dramatically—bowpickers [small boats on which the net is pulled in over the bow] and higher-speed engines, more efficient nets. As fishing became more lucrative, everything changed. People sold their permits because suddenly the permits were worth so much more. It became more difficult for women to get into the fishery at that point. You couldn't be auxiliary to your husband's operation: you either were fishing 100 percent or you weren't fishing at all. Then in '74 when fishing changed with the limited entry system, it made it more difficult for women to get in because you had to have cash up front. I was issued my permit so I stayed with it.

So all of that had a detrimental effect on women in fishing. But my folks were different. They just saw us integrated into what they were doing. My dad never left our family at home. If it meant he caught less fish, that's the way it goes. So that was cool. And then when we seined, he seined with an all-female crew, my sister, my mom, and me. My mom and my sister were on deck; I was in the jitney. So we seined a smaller boat. We seined more sheltered areas, not the capes—it was a family operation.

I have some good memories. I have some lousy ones too. Just being on a boat all summer and not having the social life of other girlfriends. Being in the skiff, with full rain gear on, it's 70 degrees, and the mosquitos are thick around your head and you're full of jellyfish. Or it's five in the morning, you just got to bed at two because you were delivering fish. But I wouldn't have had it any other way. That was great.

Cinda Gilmer

It is difficult to find something Cinda has not done. She has been an Outward Bound instructor, a carpenter, a back-country ranger, a physical education teacher, a coach, a seminary student, a model, and a commercial fisherman, to name a few. I have seen her in several of these roles and no matter how disparate they seem, each one fits her comfortably. Her busiest role to date is that of mother to her five children. She recently moved to Florida and no longer fishes commercially; her husband, Tyler, however, still commercial fishes in Alaska.

I always wanted to come to Alaska. I was teaching in Oregon at the time, then working in northern Minnesota as a permanent part-time ranger. I did that for nine summers. I was going to settle down in Minnesota and then decided, "If I don't go to Alaska now I never will." I had met this woman, Casey Janz Burns, over Spring Break on a whitewater canoeing trip. We were both in Eugene [Oregon] then, and we knew through the placement service there was a teaching job coming up here in Kodiak. I also did some research as far as where to go in Alaska to fish and kind of had narrowed it down to Kodiak or Dillingham,'cause I wanted to fish too.

We got here on the plane but our stuff didn't make it, so we didn't have any extra clothes. The first thing we did was walk the docks. I loved walking the docks. Then we walked down to Cannery Row. We were peeking in the back of Swiftsure Cannery, just looking in. Some lady says, "Oh, you want a job?" We said, "Well, we just got here. We don't have any clothes or anything." She said, "I'll give you the boots and a raincoat." We had a job by eleven o'clock that morning smacking herring [removing the roe by hand]. Then on our breaks we walked down on the docks again. I was very interested in fishing. That's what I came here to do. But I wanted to get into the right situation. And I am not a cook. I am not a cook!

After work, Casey and I walked over to the house of a friend of a friend. He was leaving for herring fishing up north. And he said we could stay at his house. We could just stay there while he was fishing. I don't know why he let us do that. We were two strangers. But here we were, first day with a job and a house to live in.

So we continued to walk the docks, but it was pretty quiet because the herring boats were all gone up north by then. When they came back we had our foot in the door. Because where we stayed the buddies of the guy whose house we were staying at came back. They were all hanging seines ["sewing" the line of corks and the line of leads to the top and bottom, respectively, of the net] to go salmon fishing. So one of the people there said he would teach us how to hang seine. He said he wouldn't pay us but he'd teach us how. And he said we could get jobs for $100 a day hanging nets. And that's exactly what we did. He hung his seine down at the harbormaster dock. So we stood there in front of everybody. Lots of people would come by and watch us. They were really scrutinizing us. He had his crewmen working too so it wasn't just us two girls standing there.

After we hung that seine for five days, we knew how. From then on I could get boat work. It was nice because there were seven of us that originally came in on that flight that morning to Kodiak, five guys and Casey and I. They were all interested in fishing. But the other guys couldn't find any work or any place to stay. That's back in the days when people just camped on the side of Pillar Mountain or down at Fort Abercrombie, in 1979. But we could already support ourselves.

We got a lot of jobs. The father of the guy who showed us how to hang seine was a fisherman from Oregon. He was a real unique guy. He'd always give Casey and me a hard time: "Oh, girls don't belong on boats." But he and I kind of hit it off, and he was the one who taught me how to mend web. They were back from herring fishing now so a lot of them were mending their seine. I just watched and seemed to have a knack for mending. I'd take web home and work on it. So I quickly learned how to mend. I worked then for Ray Wadsworth. I had to show in some way that I could work, that I had skills that would help me on a boat as compared to having to fall back on cooking. It was pretty easy to make money then.

I still wanted to fish on a boat, but I knew I had to get into the right situation. So I just tried to keep my nose clean. The other stuff seemed kind of obvious. There were stories of men taking advantage of women and I didn't want any part of that.

It was kind of hard in a lot of other ways. I wasn't into the scene that a lot of the fishing community tends to be in—the bars, the parties. I never went to the bars here. I worked, just did honest work down at the docks. And didn't really actively look for a job. Didn't say I was looking for a fishing job or anything like that. I just worked. Then in June the boats all left for reds [sockeye salmon]. And when the boats left town, I said, "I'm going to go where the boats are."

So I went to a cannery at Whitney Fidalgo on the other side of Kodiak Island and got a job on a beach gang driving a forklift and loading boats. I had a bad accident out there. Almost got my foot cut off. Then I had to go in to Kodiak to the hospital. When I was better, I flew back out and I continued to work.

And then I got a job on a boat. Basically what happened was a guy lost a crewman and I was there. He had a cook and a skiffman but he had lost his engineer. So I moved into that position. For engineer, all you have to do is change the oil. I called myself the greaser-wrencher. That I could handle. So that's how I got on there. Two of them on there were schoolteachers that I had gotten to know, so I was comfortable with that situation.

We fished into August, then fished late for silvers [salmon]. Even while we fished, we had a lot of fun. We didn't have a skipper that was a screamer. He was very confident, very experienced. We were always where the fish were. It was exciting, making these big sets. And then we did things like get a bunch of fish on the shore. We'd make a set and have to wait for the tide to go out, then stand there in the water with our hip boots, watching out for the bears, till the water came back in.

After that season, I went back Outside to teach. I came back that next summer and was at a friend's house. He said, "What are you going to do about fishing?" My skipper from last year had gotten a girlfriend by then so I knew I wouldn't go back on that boat. So I was back at square one. How do you get a job without selling yourself? That seemed like what it was back then. I mean you come as a whole package: you're a female with men. You cannot take that away. Men are men and they respond to that. The only other women I knew that were fishing had some connection, were associated with some male.

I walked down to the dock that very afternoon and Mary [Jacobs] had just fired another crewman. And so she was looking for someone and she was leaving for herring. I just talked to her. I had no hope of getting on there. I wasn't sure I even wanted to get on there. And then she called me up and said, "I'm leaving in an hour if you're interested." So I jumped on.

I went as skiffman. And that was a golden opportunity for me 'cause I'd never run a skiff. I probably would not have had that opportunity on almost any other boat, unless by accident, say someone had gotten hurt on the boat where you were the person to fill in the gap. Even the other women I've seen in the fishery, the only ones who got to run skiff, were those fishing with their spouse or their boyfriend, that kind of situation. I told her that I had never run a skiff in my life. I'd been a backcountry ranger and had been on the water, but it was in a nonmotorized area, so always a canoe and a paddle. I prayed a lot about it.

Well, I got on and it only got crazy from there. We were set gillnetting for herring. So we left town, went to Mush Bay, planted a garden for Mary, we did all this stuff. And we made kelp sets; we "fished" for kelp instead of salmon, just for practice, and for her garden. That's how I learned to run the skiff. We'd round up all this kelp, brail it on board the boat, carry it in buckets, and put it in on the garden. I'll never forget that. And I would go out there and just work in that skiff.

I had a lot of respect for Mary. I felt a lot of mutual respect from her, which I shouldn't have gotten. I didn't have any expertise or anything like that. But she treated me with a lot of dignity. She yelled at me once when we were in a really bad situation. We were by Amook Island. We made a set there and the tide was running so hard and it was dropping so fast. There were just pinnacles of rocks coming up. Our seine was out, so we were completely dependent on the skiff. And she was yelling and screaming. I said, "If you think you can do any better, get in here and do it yourself!" She jumped in the skiff and knocked the cables off the battery so we were dead in the water. Now the skiff was dead and we're both in the skiff. I put the cables back on the battery, she jumped back out, and I got us out of there. It was a bad situation. I just told her, "Screaming at me does not help me one bit." She never, never yelled at me again.

We fished with this woman who had fished previously with her husband, but they had just gotten divorced. They had two kids, and the two kids and the husband were on this other boat. So we'd see them around. But we were over on the mainland, way up north. We went in to make a set and he was there too. He came just right in front of us and laid out cork for cork and looked at us. So we backhauled our net, pulled it back in. She moved to make a set for fish coming the other direction. He started shooting at us, I mean shooting at us! He didn't hit the deck. He told us later if he wanted to hit the deck he would have, but he didn't want to. Let me tell you I'm sitting out there in my skiff, I just want to cut loose and go home. 'Cause he was crazy!

We had that little boat (twenty-nine and a half feet) that wasn't really competitive, speed or equipmentwise. The boat went like four knots. We didn't have any Loran [radar], we didn't even have a depth finder. But we stayed up all night to get places and we *were* competitive. We were where the fish were and did whatever it took. We moved over to the mainland. At that time not a lot of boats went to the mainland. When we ran from Mush Bay in to town, it would take us sixteen or twenty hours. I remember whales coming up beside us. They'd be as long as the boat, right along side of us. We were always exposed to the elements. No fresh water, no bathroom, no nothing on that boat. So it was exciting, challenging.

Mary taught me a lot. She was a hard driver. I remember one day we made like twenty-one sets for five fish. But she would not quit. She would not quit for nothing. It's hard to make twenty-one sets in a day. But I didn't mind that. It was excellent experience.

Holly Berry

Holly escaped to Alaska almost twenty years ago looking for a new life and for a way to support her young son. Her first job on a processing ship led to a string of jobs, many of them during the ten years of the king crab boom in the Bering Sea. She hired on as cook, then worked her way into deckhand.

I first started fishing in 1976 in Dutch Harbor on a processor. My husband had been killed in an accident in Seattle and I wanted to get away. It was really strange how I ended up in this place, because I'm basically a city girl. I went to school in New York, was raised in Seattle, and went to work in Seattle, had a restaurant in Seattle.

I went up to my father one night and said, "Dad, I'm really burned out on people talking about Ricky. It's over with. I'm sick of it. Where can I go?" And he took me in the den and there's a big map on the wall and he says, "I was here during the war" and he points to the Aleutian chain, which I knew nothing about at that time. And he says, "Down in Seattle, by Fishermen's Wharf, you can get a job, they'll send you to Dutch Harbor and take it out of your paycheck later. Sissy, that's how you can get out of here if you want to go somewhere and be alone."

Well, where else could you be alone more than at the end of the world? So I went to this place. It was unbelievable! We went to land and I thought we were making an emergency landing because there was no pavement or anything, just a gravel strip. It was unbelievable when I was there. And I fell in love with it. I don't know why, 'cause I wasn't raised that way, but I just fell in love with it. The thrill of surviving like that. None of the extras, just the necessities of life.

See, I had a little boy to raise, and there was nowhere I could find at that point in my life to make that much money in that short amount of time to raise him. He stayed with my parents in Seattle. I flew back and forth all the time, constantly. I sent the money home and everything was taken care of there. It was real hard on me, though: I missed him a lot. But being a cocktail waitress or something at that age I couldn't have made the money I made to take care of him.

I lived on a ship when I first got there called the *Royal Venture*. It was about four hundred feet long. It was a processing ship. I was a big girl, so they grabbed me for butchering crab in the butcher shop. And usually that's a man's job, especially in the seventies. So I clashed with a lot of the men in that situation, and that's when I learned that I liked that, that I like to compete with men.

Then I jumped on another processor, the *Denali,* run by Denali Seafoods in Seattle. The supervisor, a fifty-five-year-old man, was very, very shy. And he wanted someone who had a little bit of whatever I had. He said I had the gift to rule people all day then sit down and have dinner with them at night. So he made me a foreman on the processor just like that. I was running thirty-two kids and running the tanks and the quality control part of it too.

I was twenty-three. That was a long time ago. I wasn't the only woman on board, but I was the only woman on the top crew. The guys tried to sleep with me at first. It's like a joke you have to get through. But I don't believe in sleeping around on boats. And I never have, even when I was younger. It's the old turnaround—you do it with one, you have to do it with all. And the rules change when you get five miles out to sea. They do, they change, no matter what people say. Some of these guys get real weird. I found that intimidating them with my status and my job was the easiest way to keep them away from me. I tell them what to do, make sure what they do is correct, and if they do something wrong, I intimidate them, because I'm their boss. If you establish your authority right away like that, then they don't try anything because they're afraid of you, naturally. If you establish that on the sea, that you don't mess around, it'll run like wildfire.

I was real lucky when I started in Dutch Harbor. I got to know an old man named Buck. He was a welder, an older man, about fifty, sixty years old. And I did some work for him. I watched while he welded, made sure everything was okay. He taught me a lot about applying for jobs on boats. He's the one who really taught me, how skeptical to be, to find out their reputation on the water, find out how they run the vessel. All these things he taught me that sunk in greatly.

When I was younger I used to go down and hit the docks, they call it, walk the docks. You'd get on boats and you'd talk to guys and you'd talk to the skipper. Then when the skipper disappears and you're sitting with the crew, the crew will do a flip-flop the minute he leaves, like a card. They become themselves. And that's who you're really cooking for and dealing for and handling and sewing for and washing for and all these things that you do for these men and run deck, on top of everything else. They're the ones. Not him. He sits upstairs.

So I interview them, the crew. I can tell by the things they want to eat, how uppity they get about food, how quick-tempered they become while I'm speaking to them how quick-tempered they might become when something happens out there. My life might be in their hands.

When you're the cook, you're doing so much more than cooking. You're literally running their lives. You're feeding them, taking care of them, making their beds; you're the psychiatrist. When one of them's upset, you're the one who gets woke up. You do everything. Basically they're little boys in big men's bodies.

There's this little area in the galley, and when fishing is slow, there could be five or six of them running circles around you. So I'd chalk the floor around the galley. If they cross the mark, they don't get dinner. They're just like fathers—they want to come in and smell everything and cut everything and dip into everything. You know, eat half the cookie dough before it's baked, all that kind of stuff. But when we hit the crab and they yell, "Crab's on!" and they go out that door, that's when they become the men they are—doing the most dangerous job in the world, as far as I'm concerned.

But I worked on deck, too. Just like the men, I got addicted to what they called "crab fever." I would never have thought even in my wildest nightmares in the old days when I was married that I would ever do anything like I did—running a crew, running hydraulics out on deck, running a crane, baiting jars [pots], everything. But you just wake up one day and you're in a position on a boat or working on deck and the weather's bad and this problem has to be solved and you do it. Then an hour later you say, "Wow! I did this! I can do this! I can do this again and I can make more money and I can do it just as good as he can!"

There are moments when you're going along at night across miles of sea with nothing in sight—my gosh, unbelievably beautiful! The neatest feeling is just knowing that no one in the whole world knows where you are at that very moment. That's what I liked.

2 *"People Don't Work Like This"*

JULY 21, 1980, BEAR ISLAND

From the moment I stepped into the skiff with Duncan and DeWitt today, we did nothing but pick fish frantically—the nets were all full and then some. I picked almost as fast as Duncan, and DeWitt was tired, so he was slower. We picked 1,600 fish in just a short time. By the time we finished up with those, with aching backs that begged "no more!" we did the rest of those nets in the dark, then went on down to the nets at Seven-Mile. It seemed it would never end. I don't like working in the dark. Sometimes we can barely see where we are going. Even so, the picking fish went on, still furious, but we were all wearing out. By the time we finished those nets and delivered the fish to the tender, we didn't get home until 2:00 A.M. My left arm aches and my hands are burning from being constantly wet with saltwater. The skin has peeled away to raw red underneath that sometimes bleeds. I have to wrap my fingers every morning with adhesive tape now before I go out.

I remember this first and most about fishing: commercial fishing is a verb and the verb is "work." On my first trip to Alaska, my let-me-see-what-I'm-getting-into-before-I-get-married trip, I got a full, clear view of what life as a fisherman was like: I never stopped working the entire ten days. No one else did either. It was the end of the salmon season, and Duncan's family—his mother, father, two brothers, and sister-in-law, and now me, the prospective addition to this island family—frantically worked to put away all the gear and close up the whole camp for the winter before the fierce September blows came. We stopped only one day to leap, screaming, into the forty-three-degree ocean for a swim and a surreptitious test of my East Coast mettle. But the visit was not some kind of elaborately devised test; it was simply the way one lives out on a fish site where the work defines the day, and I knew that, even then.

Like everyone else there, we work following the long summer light, the tides, the direction of the winds, the openings and closures of the fishing seasons. That translates to a schedule like this: during our salmon season we work twelve to eighteen hours a day seven days a week from May 20 to September 20. We take the Fourth of July off, and if fishing is slow and the weather is good, we may end early on occasional evenings, at 9:00 or 10:00 P.M., and have a wiener roast on the beach and play "shinny," a crude version of hockey using driftwood for a stick and a tin can for the puck— vacation, weekend, and recreation compressed into one evening.

Some fishermen don't work as hard. Others work harder. We worked with one fishing family last summer who thought us lazy. Theresa Peterson fishes cod on draggers (boats that drag the bottom of the water for fish) and routinely works twenty-four-hour shifts before taking three hours off for sleep. Three hours up and the next twenty-four-hour shift begins. And this she thought was reasonable compared to other boats' schedules.

But the work is often cyclical. No one can sustain those hours or that kind of labor without a stoppage or breakdown. For salmon fishermen, the season generally lasts as long as the fish are running. For setnetters and seiners around Kodiak Island, salmon fishing runs from June through September. In some places in Alaska, the season is much shorter, just six weeks in Bristol Bay—short and oh so fleet! It's a boom-and-bust pattern that we in the North and Northwest know so well—the gold rush of the Klondike, the Alaska oil boom of the 1970s, the frenzy of seasonal fishing, logging, and mining—delirious activity followed by a sudden quiet. But it is *hard to generalize about the seasons and times of work for all who fish. Some are salmon fishermen who work only in the summers, as we do; others fish year round, doing cod, halibut, herring, crab, each a distinct fishery with its own schedules and regulations; others work at two or three fisheries. And there is any combination of the above. But even for those who fish through the year, the boom-and-bust cycle holds true. There can be weeks, even months between seasons and fishing trips.*

Seasons and duration of work are only part of it. What most people really want to know is "How hard is the work?" And when and if they ask me or other women who fish, they may look sidelong and disbelieving, depending on how big we are. Debbie Nielsen is 5' and 100 pounds. Christine Holmes is 5'2" and 110 pounds: both get the shocked, assessing looks all the time. I know about those looks too; I'm about the same size. And though many times I have envied just the sheer weight and mass and musculature of the men I was working with, I have never felt small or weak. Neither has Christine: "This isn't a real ladylike fishery. You have to grunt, you have to make noises like 'Yeaaahhh! Grab that baby and hold down the deck!' When I'm fishing I'm 6'4". I really think I am. I have this image of myself, and sometimes guys would say, 'God, you act like you're 6'4".'"

Strength and size is important, of course. But in this chapter you will hear these women talk much more about endurance, about technique, about speed and skill, about wanting to work.

Clearly, for many women, the work itself is a means to an end: For Theresa Peterson, the means to paying off a house and boat mortgage; for Laurie Jolly and Rebecque Raigoza, the means to paying off school debts; for Lisa Jakubowski, a means of financing nursing school so she can quit fishing; and for Christine Holmes, a means of simply earning her own living—she expects to make six figures this year. Occasionally there is someone like Martha Sutro who crab fishes in the Bering Sea as a means of—crab fishing in the Bering Sea. For her, the work is the reason for working.

Theresa Peterson

Theresa has fished nearly ten years, catching everything from salmon to herring, and spent many years long-lining—working miles-long fishing

lines with many hooks. When we met for coffee last spring, she was pre-
paring to go out for another black cod season. She was in an enviable di-
lemma: she had to choose between several offers from highline skippers—
the most successful fishermen—who knew of her reputation as one of the
fastest baiters in the fleet. That reputation led to jobs with work schedules
that were inhuman, at best. The almost maniacal intensity Theresa de-
scribes here is changing, however, with a new system of regulations (IFQs)
that lengthens the season and reduces the competitive pressure.

The last black cod season started May 15. It was two gals and two guys.
The skipper wanted a crew that could bait gear fast; that was what he
was looking for. He heard that both Lisa [Jakubowski] and I were real
fast baiters. He had sought everyone out and was trying to put together
a crew that was all very experienced. He wanted to run a lot more gear
than he had been able to run the year before.

To start out, all we were trying to do is turn hooks. It's a numbers
game. Ideally you run 18,000–20,000 hooks a day. And so we'd have
four people baiting at all times and one person hauling gear. The people baiting would rotate coiling the gear. We went back to the traditional way of fishing. Most Kodiak boats will let the gear fall into a tub,
kind of on its own, then you bring that tub back and bait it. On the
old halibut schooners they hand coil everything so they're able to off-
spin every hook. They try to make a really nice coil so when you take
it back you can bait it twice as fast. Those first couple of days we looked
at the time it was taking to bait the messy skates [the long lines on
which the hooks are attached]. I refused to bait another skate like that,
so then we all started hand coiling our own. When you do that you're
able to move from your baiting station. We really worked long hours,
often twenty-four hours, then we go into the next day and work
through that night till about 2:00 A.M. and the next day another twenty
hours. Then we'd lie down for about three hours. Then we'd get back
up and go another twenty-four hours and a couple hours down. The
first week we averaged ten hours of sleep all together—we figured it
out. So we joked, twenty-four on, one off.

I had never fished that hard before. When it opened, we fished Saturday, all through Saturday, all through Sunday, and half of Monday,
so well over fifty-six hours with no sleep, working as hard, as fast, as

high paced as you can push yourself. Then we laid down for like three hours. You get up, you are so stiff! Then we brought in a trip, just over 40,000 pounds in four days, so we virtually had been up those entire four days. That was a good load. It was really motivational. I made a thousand dollars a day. So I would remind myself of that.

Then we headed back out and baited all the way out to the grounds so we had our gear ready to set. Then we went another two days straight, fishing. Lisa and I were both hearing things and seeing things. I'd go in to cook and hear them yelling "Buoy!" 'cause that meant it was time to pick up the gear and I'd run back out there and there would be nothing there. I'd hear "Flag!" "Gear!" just kind of going delirious. Lisa came out on deck. I saw her looking at something and going and picking it up real carefully. Well, it was the gill of a black cod that she thought was a bird. We looked at each other—we couldn't believe it. We just kept drinking coffee, coffee, ten to twelve cups a day to try to keep going.

As it turned out, we were trying to run 18,000–20,000 hooks a day but we were all so fatigued that we just couldn't go to full capacity anymore. So after seven days of working almost continuously, we laid down for about five or six hours, then throughout the rest of the season, another two weeks, we'd work between twenty and twenty-two hours, then lay down for between two and four hours. And that was for the duration of the season. After the first trip, I thought the pace would slow down, but it didn't. A couple of times when I was coiling, I nodded out and fell asleep—it was getting dangerous to try to work those hours. So I had decided I was going to get off the boat. I found myself coming into the galley and looking at the pictures of my kids thinking, "I'll make it back to you somehow!" That's when I thought this whole thing was ridiculous. But that's when the skipper recognized he had pushed his crew to the limit, and that's kind of being the hard-driving, highliner skipper. He saw just how far we could go, then he turned it down a notch. He was falling asleep too. I saw him out there. He dressed [gutted] all the fish. He really worked hard right there with us. But three fish in a row he threw the head in the fish hold and threw the body over the side; then he realized what he was doing. He went "okay!" but we were all nodding out. I would see him go up in the chair [up in the wheelhouse]; it's so warm up there he'd just be dropping down in ten minutes.

It's the shorter seasons, the shorter longline seasons, are what are driving the boats back to these schedules. When I long-lined, we never put in long hours like that. We worked long days, twenty-hour days back in the eighties, but we didn't work around the clock day in and day out. With a three-week season, you're almost forced to unless you can rotate a person down [let them sleep].

After this second black cod trip, the skipper very much wants me to come back. I'm not sure if I want to. We ran a lot of gear, 250 skates, so everything had to be full steam. There are quite a few boats out there, so it's real heavy pressure.

Long-lining black cod, I was always able to do everything men were able to do. In crabbing, I don't think I would ever be able to compete with some of the guys. I realized that when we fished the black cod pots [steel and nylon web cages]. I'd be up at the rail trying to land them. I'd bring it in, then we'd take a big swell and I could tell that either that pot was going to pull me over or I had to let go. So I had to let go and then it would fly up in the air and come back down. It was just physically a little bit too much for me. They weren't that big, 130 pounds, probably. They were just beyond my capacity. And the halibut, it is so difficult to get some of those big fish on the hatch. I'll work with other guys and they'll see it's just their physical strength that comes in handy when you're dealing with the big fish. With the black cod, most of it is speed and endurance. You're continually pushing yourself in order to keep turning that gear. You're baiting, baiting, just as fast as you can. This last trip we were the top boat in all of Alaska out of 170 boats.

There was a great sense of fulfillment knowing how much we could use this money. When I fished in the eighties, I didn't have any children, a home, mortgages, or boat payments. So I was making a lot of money, but it just wasn't as important to me as it is now.

We had a young man from Virginia on board, a college student, who came up and said, "You know, back in Virginia they would never believe me when I say the people work like they do up here. A fifteen-hour day is a pretty long day, eighteen hours, but you guys work around the clock, twenty-four hours. People don't work like this in other parts of the world." It's a rarity and it's part of the great Alaskan fishing tradition. To be a part of it is pretty special to me.

Leslie Smith

Leslie started fishing on a salmon purse seining boat around Kodiak Island. In purse seining, the net is set by two vessels, a larger boat and a skiff. The net is gradually brought into a circle and the bottom of the net is pursed shut, entrapping the fish. She crewed for a few seasons, then bought and skippered her own seine boat until her two daughters were born. Rather than give up fishing, she switched to setnetting. Her site on the west side of Kodiak on the Shelikof Strait, where she lives with her two preschool daughters and three hired crew members, is known as one of the roughest around the island.

I seined with Mary Jacobs all one summer. At the end of summer she tried me out for skiffman, but she didn't tell me what to do. She just said, "Get in the skiff!" And it was a new job, it's a hard job. You need to figure it out. It's nice to have someone tell you a few things, like do this, do that, turn the kicker [motor] in the opposite direction because you're towing a net and you have to steer the opposite way to get the net to go where you want it to go. You know, really simple things like that. So I had to figure it out myself. And I was screwing up like anybody.

I remember the first time I was in the skiff. We were at Packer's Spit. I was towing the net on the beach. I wasn't close enough to the beach and she wanted me to be right on the beach. But being new at it I didn't feel like driving right up into the breakers. She was apparently standing on deck yelling at me, which is the classic thing because you can't hear the skipper from the skiff. We didn't have radios back then, and this huge outboard was running full bore. I was kind of looking at her—I was basically just trying to do what the skiffman is supposed to do: keep the net out of the propeller and the boat out of the breakers. She was jumping up and down on the hatch covers, being angry with me. She had this guy as crewman who was some friend of her ex-husband's. And he just couldn't stand the sound of her voice because she has kind of a shrill voice when she gets excited. So I'm watching and the next thing I saw was he had her down on the hatch covers and was lying on top of her strangling her. I thought, "Oh my god, now what do I do?" The only other person on the boat was this teenager who was the guy's son and he was just standing there. So I'm thinking, "Oh shit! What do I do? The skipper's being strangled!" By then I think I had decided to go rescue her, but I got web in the wheel so I was all screwed up; I was out of commission. The guy had a big beard, though, so Mary grabbed his beard and started yanking on it and she ended up rescuing herself. After that it was, "Okay, we're going to town right now." That was the end of the season. She drove the boat from the inside cabin and he drove the boat from the flying bridge. They were both driving the boat all the way to town. They wouldn't talk to each other.

But the reason I feel lucky is because we were out there, a woman running a boat with an all-women crew, and we were doing it. And we were doing it as well as anybody else in the fleet, so I never felt intimidated in thinking, "Oh, a woman can't do this, can't figure it out, or is not capable of it" because the first job I ever had was with women and we did fine. So I had that confidence factor from the beginning of my deckhand career. I didn't see anything more difficult, except fishing crab in the Bering Sea, but I wasn't interested in that. So it was a good place to start.

I really liked seining because it was a real challenge; you can be constantly challenged. That's what it is. You can always get better at it. That's the thing that really attracted me to seining: I felt like no matter how long I did it, I could always get better at it. But I never got to test that out because I quit seining to start a family. When I started having babies, I got into this whole maternal mode. It's really kind of an opposite thing. I don't really care about being a predator. I'm in a nurturing role right now. They're kind of opposite ways of being. Not that you couldn't do it, I guess, but I've lost interest in that.

I never was one of these people that was ultracompetitive. I really enjoyed it and liked being out there, and if I could make a living at it, I'd be happy. But there's a lot of guys out there that are determined to be the best. And they're good. Those are the guys that are really making it. They're the assholes, the cutthroats, they'll do anything to you to get the fish. They won't ram you so much, but they'll cork you [set their net in front of yours]. Seining has this whole elaborate structure of unwritten rules. There's lots of ways to violate the little code of ethics. It's hard to describe unless you're out there because it wouldn't mean anything. "Well, he put his net here and it's supposed to be there" and you know if he did it on purpose or not. And everyone's so close to each other seining, taking turns in very specific spots. If you screw up your timing, then you screw up the guy who's going next. It's a very psychological thing. It's not like you're fishing out on the open sea all by yourself, just you and the fish. It's really you and all the other guys competing for those fish.

When you're on a boat you don't have a life, you don't have any physical space, you don't have any time to yourself. It's all the boat, the fishing, for four months straight. You get really burned out. I see it happening with my husband now, and I don't envy him at all. I'm a setnetter now. Actually when we first met, in 1985, I was a seiner and he was a setnetter. But he was sick of setnetting, so we talked about it and that year he traded his setnet permit for a seine boat and permit, an even-up trade. And he's evolved into a seiner, a good seiner since then, and I'm a setnetter now!

This was my first year setnetting, and actually it went really well. I've had enough experience with crew and fishing that I didn't really anticipate it being a problem. I ran a seiner for three years. And I thought, "This shouldn't be harder than seining, it should be easier." And it was in some ways. There are a lot of differences between seining and setnetting. Setnetting is a lot harder work physically. It's a lot more just nitty-gritty, down-and-dirty work. You're just out there with your hands picking individual pieces of kelp. Seining you've got hydraulics. But the big thing that makes fishing easier in setnetting is that you really don't have to figure out how to catch the fish or where the fish are. Seining, to me, that was the most difficult, just trying to be in the right place at the right time. Also when you're seining, your net is this fluid dynamic thing that's changing all the time, so the way you handle your net is determining how much fish you catch. Setnetting it's a little more simple. I sort of liken it to having this little fence and you stick it out there in the water and the fish crash into it. It's a little more complicated than that, but not much.

Chasing the fish was a real agony for me. I didn't seine for enough years to really feel like I had a grip on that. I crewed on seine boats for three years before I bought one, and I knew enough to know it takes five to ten years for people to really get a good handle on it. I did a lot of just following other boats around and wondering if I was in the right place. It's a huge area to fish, Kodiak Island, and there are so many different places to go. You watch the old timers and try to figure them out—why they're going where they're going and when—it's really an art. But in the beginning it's a guessing game. After ten years or so, even if you don't have a log book that you can refer to, you have it all in your mind. People operate on instinct. "I have a feeling I should go over there, it's about that time of year . . ." But I never got to that point.

But then on the other hand, the actual work is a lot easier on a seiner, the physical part. There's much more work to do on a setnet site. Everyone says my site is one of the toughest on Kodiak, but really I'm getting the same waves that everybody else is getting; it's just that at my site I get all of them. Most people are protected from at least one or two wind directions, so they may be okay on a northeast or a southwest blow, but I just don't have that protection. I have a little bit of protection on some of the winds, but pretty much I'll get all of it. So it gets kind of old. It's just the wind and the waves. Cape Ugat, just south of my site, is a really windy spot. I'll go out there sometimes and it'll be just howling, but it won't be in the rest of the Shelikof. I'll talk to Kay and Andy around the corner and it'll be flat calm there. It's the narrowest part of the Shelikof Strait, so there's a bit of a wind tunnel there. It's not a big swell, but you pull up to grab ahold of the line, and you can just barely get the line in the skiff. There's also a lot of tide here. You dump these anchors off; you've got fifteen or twenty anchors, some of them three hundred pounders, to try and hold one net in place. And every time you go out there the net's twisted in some different shape and you have to drag these anchors around. And the weather is not very nice most of the time. You're just always fighting the wind. It's a challenge, a physical challenge instead of a mental challenge. So that's not really what I thought I'd be doing. I don't really need a physical challenge. I would enjoy a mental challenge more. But it's the only kind of fishing you can do and have your family there.

If I could work it so I had good people to work for me that could go out and do everything, I would stay off the water more. And I ended up with a good crew this summer. Actually I started the season out with two guys that were just awful. I picked them independently of each other and they were two of the worst people I've ever had. I had them there for the first opening in June. It was so horrible I just brought them back to town. One of them was nineteen and I hired him because he said he could carry a forty-horse outboard—that's the kind of guy I needed. And he had some setnet experience. But he had some real emotional problems. Kind of a bad egg. So then I hired this older guy who's thirty-four, figuring the older guy would guide the younger one, because the younger one turned out to have no judgment-making capabilities. So I thought the older one would be the leader, but it turned out that he was really quiet and would never speak up. He ended up doing what the nineteen year old suggested. It was just a very bad combination. Unbelievably bad.

In the beginning of the season, it was me and these two guys. We did the halibut opening and then had to get ready for the salmon season. I had to set up all these salmon sets, had to drop the anchors in just the right places. I didn't know what I was doing! "Oh, throw the anchors out and I guess we tie up to this rock here . . ." And so it was kind of hard because we'd end up having to do things a few times over. They'd think I was an idiot because I didn't do it right the first time. I said, "Hey, I told you guys all along that I haven't done this before and that we'll be learning together. I appreciate whatever input you have, blah, blah, blah . . ." And the young guy took that to mean that I was completely green and didn't know anything about fishing and started treating me that way. Here's this nineteen-year-old kid telling me, "You're green. I've fished before, but you're green." He had this attitude and it obviously was not working out for me.

I had this third crew member, a gal, who was green. She was a cabaret singer from Minneapolis. She had the best attitude of anyone. She really tried hard. She wasn't very big or strong and had never fished, but she had a great attitude all summer, always joking in the skiff or whenever. She was also helping with the kids in the beginning, because I didn't get my babysitter until July.

I ended up firing the older guy because he just started getting weird. They found a puffin in the net and the cabaret singer gal, who's this New Age kind of person, was all upset because this puffin was dead. And he thought it would be great to cut off the puffin's head and hang it over her bed. He thought that was funny. And I thought that was a good reason to send him back to town. You're thirty-four years old and you're doing this kind of shit, you know, maybe you better go do it somewhere else.

I'd never setnetted before, so we did a lot of things the hard way, the wrong way. And there were so many things—you go out and your net is just full of kelp or popweed and the only thing you can do is pick it out by hand. It takes hours and hours. Sometimes I can't believe I'm doing this. It's just so labor intensive. It really is. By the end of the season I felt like, "Oh I just don't want to go out there. You guys go out there." And I felt kind of bad. But I know some people that never go out on their nets. I've heard of them. Sometimes I'd like to be more like them. But then I feel guilty. And if you've got a crew you have to work side by side with them to instill them with the standard you want to uphold. You can't expect them to do what you want them to do. You have to be there and do it with them.

Sometimes I can't believe I'm taking this step in my life from what I've been doing. Setnetting is so manual, so Neanderthal. It's like I'm going backwards. I'm supposed to be evolving, but all of a sudden I'm out here just doing this primitive, time-consuming work. But it makes you feel alive, I guess. I mean, I like being out there; I like the lifestyle, but the actual work sometimes makes me wonder.

Martha Sutro

I got a call one day on the radiophone while I was out at fish camp—it was Martha Sutro, a woman who had been crabbing the previous winter in the Bering Sea. Because there are so few women winter fishing, I was anxious to meet her and all the more so after I found out she was a writer and an English teacher. By chance, her boat was in Kodiak for repairs. Three hours, a bush plane flight, and a skiff ride later, Martha was at our remote fish camp and we were shut in a back room with the tape player running.

Even in the daily things in crabbing I felt stress. You had to get out on deck, you had to get your gear right, you were working hard. You had to just be ready. People would yell at you, there was just a great urgency when you were on the crab. Getting it out of the pots. You're either baiting the pots or putting them back in. It's tough. There's a lot of running around. The lines are everywhere. The danger of it is so apparent. I felt it so strongly when the pot goes in the water because there's this tremendous rush. I felt the weight of the pot. I would have dreams about this too. I would dream about sorting crab—suddenly the crab were too big for me to handle and I'd see crab on the pillow, crab on the floor, crab on Doug who's sleeping above me, and cod that were too big to handle, you know, going crazy, saying, "I can get this one!" You know when they stack the pots with a crane on deck? I had dreams, too, about being in between two pots. And they were bringing a pot down to fit in the hole I was in. I had that dream all the time. It was terrible.

One night we were working on deck and it was the only time I really felt fearful. The weather got pretty rough. I was sorting crab near the aft hole and a wave came and hit me from the back and just put me down on my knees. I was looking in the face of bardai [crab]. "Oh wow, that was kind of strong," I thought. I was getting up. The boys were back by the shelter deck; they had kind of been shaken a little bit, too. I saw them working back there—it was just my second week working on the deck—and I knew they were going to be wondering how that was handled. No one, of course, says, "Are you okay?" I love the understatement. There's no limit to the subtlety, I love that. I got up and said, "Um, that felt pretty good." It's such a game of subtlety, you don't go back there with this grin on your face and you don't go back there like "Ahhh! I had a terrible time at the aft hole!" You just go back, the messages are all said, everything's all sealed up. Then Jeff got on the hailer [external intercom] and said, "It's a little rough, let's come in." But I didn't feel fearful for my life then, it's just—"I'm not on my feet."

Yeah, the intricacies of this kind of communication are interesting, and how you are met with approval. I mean there was never anyone who signaled that you are approved of or disapproved of. Nobody came forth and made any statement, not Jeff, Mike, the guy who ran the crane—nobody—and I was just Captain Feedback. I go in there the teacher—"You're doing that pretty well. You're not running the crane very well. You made a mistake—better go back to the wheelhouse!" I really look for it in my own way, as much as wanting to give it out, but I would never tell these guys how they did things. On the deck things were pretty much straight shot, clear. It's just no one's going to turn around and say, "You're wonderful. You did such a wonderful job." You get the job done.

There's no integrating going on, though. It's like—objective, objective, objective—task-solution, task-solution. Like the buoy is in your hands and you almost have the knot right and it's going to be so important that you learn the knot so the next time you can dash through the knot and throw the buoy over with the pot, but they'll rip it out of your hand. And it's not necessarily their abruptness that bothers you, although that does bother me too. It's the fact that if they would see that I was about to get it, and if I get it they'll never have to rip it out of my hand again ever, but they stopped me in the midst of learning what I was about to learn. Those little things—no one is integrating here.

And as far as enjoying the process too. There were times I was relishing a beautiful sight or something incredible that came up in the pot. There's this one asshole on the boat who was really quite a funny character, but as far as not integrating, he was completely cut off. I remember a couple of times these little baby squids would come up or these big octopi. Around the Pribs [Pribilof Islands] in the spring were just all these multicolored fish, all this gorgeous stuff coming up in the pots. And every time it came up it was just so great. And there was no one else to say, "Yes! It's great! There are no crab in that pot, but it's beautiful." When you're setting out at night and there's a storm coming up. You're out of Dutch Harbor; there's spray on the windows; it's black outside. You think, "It's great! This in itself is great!" But there was no one else on the crew who adores that. No one had that appreciation. After awhile you were just like, "I love this, but I feel so alone in the way I am loving it." It's not like you were miserable, but you miss that, the way that women very easily have an affinity with the process instead of the price, and when you're going to get there and . . .

There were these spaces of silence. You'd be working, everyone would be really into the work. I would think, "We can do more than just work here. We can be having incredible conversations at this very moment. There are no phones, there's no radio to interrupt us." And that's when I would miss my friends because I have some friends that would love that work. They would love that work, but they would be able to talk about something that wasn't even deep or hard or difficult or anything, but here's a story of what you did when you were four or what you're going to do when you're fifty. Who cares? The dream you had last night. But that strain is what creates that loneliness. Someone gave me this Carolyn Forché poem. She speaks in the first person, it's like first-person omniscient; she's aware of everything. Isn't that like the female experience? Like constantly bathing in empathy. It's like you're here and you're there and you're there and you're everywhere, and you can talk, you can do . . . It's like women in the kitchen. They're talking, the kids are going, they're watching TV.

This kind of work is almost like a haven for men. They can be exactly that way, definitively that way. It can be very calming, but you have to be at peace when you're there doing it and be content with the silences.

In a way I liked it that there were no women there. I like being able to enter the world of men and, you know, exist, and breathe and prosper. It makes you feel like you don't have that constant need for relationship, although when you're off the boat you're on the phone immediately. But as much as I think we appreciate the way women integrate things, and they do combine a million things together when they work, there is something about male psychology that's very defined, very pure. It's evidenced very clearly. And I feel like being able to draw on that part of me that's there. Sometimes by the fifth day it's very frustrating because you haven't had a satisfying conversation in all those days. But then there are other times when you can boil yourself down to an action, to an act. It's nice to work on deck—you don't have to worry about anything. You don't think about anything. You're just out here to do this. Every once in a while it's very easy, very calming. Such an easy thing to do. It's like this is the task for the day: I'm going to put these pots in the water. It's not like teaching at all, of course. I didn't invest myself in this work in the same way I did in teaching. I felt incredibly interested in crabbing and I felt incredibly aligned with the work, but I didn't feel a great compassion for it and I felt a great compassion for teaching. And I felt a great compassion for the process of learning.

To satisfy my creativity on the boat, I made a lot of bread. I learned how to play chess. I learned a lot about how to drive a boat, how to change the oil, switch generators. I just saw it as a chance, like, "I can learn about this whole other world"—how to tie that knot, how to fix the pot, what species that is . . . I'm too much of an anthropologist to not do that. I love taking that approach, just treating this like a museum. God, you get to live in this museum! You get to touch everything and be with everything. It's just so rare that you can stretch this and step out of one world and into another. Just put on a hat and a slicker and a pair of rain boots and suddenly you're not who you were. It's like masquerade, like Virginia Woolf. It's just like suddenly you're a man for four months. I mean for a lot of intents and purposes, you are. I love doing that kind of stuff, so it wasn't an identity crisis; it was more like an identity playground. And I felt very secure doing it.

When I first considered fishing, I was working in Vermont. I was thinking of leaving teaching. I wanted to go to the South Pole and I wanted to go to Asia and I wanted to go fishing. I called up my friend Jeff and he said you can definitely go fishing, but it's going to be really hard. He said they were batting ice off with big bats—it was tough going the first months. He sent me a video of the guys beating the ice off the boat. I wanted to see the Bering Sea in winter. I was like, "There's no reason to be forbidden from seeing that." I guess it was sort of an "I'm-going-to-get-there-Goddammit. If it's dangerous and it's hard, I'm going," which is sort of typical mode of reaction for me. Also on the same video there were incredible whales, the sea going up and down. Everything was just gray—it was beautiful. The whole sky was gray, there was floating ice, and the whole sea was just breathing. And the boat's just sitting on there looking for buoys. I was like, "I've got to go! That's accessible to me; I'm free to go. Why don't I go? I thought, "If those people can go out there and see all that . . ." Yeah, they have to bat the ice off, that's trouble, but I really wanted to see it. I don't think Jeff had romanticized it, but he had such a deep appreciation for it. I mean, here we are on this planet. I just feel like it's what we owe ourselves: work on the land, work on the sea. Climb the mountains, swim the rivers. I don't even feel like it's the Ten Commandments; I just feel like it's available to you. Why wouldn't you want to do that? My mother can think of quite a few reasons why I wouldn't want to do it, but I just really didn't care that it's dirty, that the boat is a dirty place, and that I slept in this little bunk.

We took the boat down south. I had a couple friends going to college in Seattle. I took them down and showed them the boat. They had a very honest, real reaction to it. They said, "God, everything is just so dirty!" You know how ugly those boats are. It had just been out the whole spring. The galley was a mess, everything was just really used up. They were just like, "How did you deal with this?" I was just, "I loved it!" I loved being enclosed like that and getting up for watch. Driving the boat in the middle of the night—it's one of the most powerful memories of being on watch alone in the dark with all those lights on the panel, everyone's asleep, the radar's just going around. I loved it, too, when we drove south and there was navigating to do. Just putting that puzzle together, looking on the chart, seeing how many times it [the navigational light] should blink, and just doing all this really quietly in the night by yourself. Having this huge boat that's just whummmmmm! And the birds. The birds around St. George in the sodium lights. I just always remember the birds.

I was thinking about the question you asked earlier, why women are increasingly drawn to this. I don't know. You wonder if there are increasing numbers of women coal mining or trucking. I don't know if it has to do with Alaska and the whole lure of being able to partake of something that formerly was withheld from you or maybe it's a breed of women who have been raised or have somehow grown up to understand that certain barriers that supposedly were there are not legitimate. Even withstanding all the dangers, it's an important experience and it's very viable, very—I hate to use the word "fulfilling," but it is very fulfilling. I loved, I *loved* getting a string of pots over perfectly and not having to ask anyone to help me with one of the doors once and getting all the massive wads of bait that you sort of swoop under the pot in the middle. You know, if I could do that perfectly on a string, I felt like that was great. What an accomplishment! Aren't I great? And isn't this great? Fulfillment was everywhere. There are elements to it you can't find in any other type of experience. It's almost like farming. It's so elemental. It calls on such an elemental process. Since biblical times we've been talking about these kind of people. There's this ethos surrounding it that's very ancient. And to be able to go to that and draw on it. It gets into this whole mystical realm.

Laurie Jolly and Rebecque Raigoza

Last summer an ungainly entourage stopped at a beach near my fish site in Uyak Bay: three people in full orange rain gear running two skiffs and a jitney, an old-style wooden boat. It wasn't the rain gear that was strange—all fishermen wear it—or that this obviously was a beach seining operation, a moveable fleet—even though there aren't many of them around. There was something else. I couldn't see form or face, but somehow I knew that at least one of the three was a woman. As it turned out, two were women: Laurie Jolly and Rebecque Raigoza, both recent college graduates from Santa Barbara, who were beach seining together for their second year.

Rebecque: When Laurie said she was going to Alaska to visit her friend and try to get a job out of it I said, "Wow, this is really cool!" 'cause I wanted to go to Alaska and make my money. So the fireball just started rolling. We were both going together. For me it was very comforting to have someone to go with. It was hard to just take off and do something like that by yourself. We were going to have a place to stay 'cause her friend was house sitting. There was a minimal amount of insecurity involved. Otherwise, I don't know if I could have just come.

Laurie: I just graduated from UC Santa Barbara and I was trying to put myself through. It's taken me six years to get through. I had to take a couple of years off at first because I didn't qualify for financial aid. So I needed to make some money.

I wouldn't have come up here if I didn't have my friend up here. It worked out great because I always wanted to come to Alaska. Everything I've seen of it is so gorgeous.

I didn't really know anything about commercial fishing before I came up. I was walking the docks and met this other guy who was walking the docks and he showed me the difference between tender boats and seining boats. He asked me what kind of job I wanted to get and if I wanted to go tendering or seining. I didn't know. I did try to get a job on a tender because they did make so much money that was guaranteed, but I'm really glad that things worked out the way they did.

We didn't catch very much that first year beach seining, but we got the experience and learned everything we needed to know. But I didn't feel everything was complete, so I felt I had to come up here again and prove to myself and my family that I could fish, that I didn't just fail.

Rebecque: Before this, Laurie and I met at a restaurant and fish market. We were both the only young women there to do delivery work around town. For me that was nontraditional. I felt like I was the only gal with Laurie doing the men's work.

Laurie: We'd always get reactions like, "Oh, a woman!" Surprise, surprise! When I was in high school I worked at a fish and poultry market. People were always surprised. I had a couple of older gentlemen who weren't really into it. They'd say, "I'll wait for Al." I'd say, "Fine. I can quarter the chicken better, but that's all right."

In a way we get treated really nicely. Some of the guys, the seiners even, will come up and talk to us. Some of the tenders say, "Oh, you're our favorite delivery." But sometimes it's like we're getting negative comments because we're fishers. Because we're women, how can we possibly get anything done? And especially with two women. Sometimes they'll make insinuations, for instance, if we can't get the skiff started or tying off or we make a mistake. I feel like everyone's watching me and I want to tie the correct knot. They'll say, "Here, just hand me that line, I'll do it." They're knocking me down rather than just saying, "This is how you do it" or "Let me show you." Maybe they assume you can't do it.

And last summer we were in town and had an encounter with a couple of people. These Russian fishers were saying lewd things to us. Just a few minutes later we had some Filipino guys saying nasty things to us. We were just sitting outside eating french fries between the Mecca and Henry's Bar. It must have been a weekend night or something. Everyone was partying but we were hungry, as beach seiners usually are. So we got some french fries and were just sitting out on the stairs, enjoying the night, talking, not doing anything, and we got approached. I just looked at them and said, "We're here to fish, we're fishers, and we happen to be women like your mothers are women. You respect your mothers, so please respect me, because I'm just here to work. I don't want this kind of treatment. I'm not a sex object. I have these boots on because I'm a fisher, not because I'm a sleaze or whatever you want me to be." They both stopped and left. The Filipino guy apologized.

Last year we had warning shots fired at us. We were down in Zacher Bay looking for a place to fish. We'd been fishing but it was slow. We were just tooling around. We had gone to this beach just to check it out and were leaving and this seiner that was nearby, he fired ten rounds at the beach that we were at. We said, "Let's get out of here!" But then the guy we were fishing with knew the boat was trying to scare us off. We had heard stories about people getting shot off their bows in the old days. So we started taking off really fast, but then our skipper stopped and said, "On behalf of all beach seiners, I have to go back and confront this man." We would never cork anyone. We know how to play the game. So he went back and tried to talk to the skipper of the boat. At first the skipper tried to say he was shooting at a fox on the beach but then he admitted that he was trying to make it clear that that was his territory, which is ridiculous. We've been taking turns with all the other fishermen without any problems.

A funny thing about that was, maybe a week later, we were at camp, Ed, Rebecque, and I. It was night, dark out. We heard some guys walking up the beach. They had rifles and were in full rain gear. We thought, "What's going on?" Ed's real friendly, says, "Hi, how are you?" They had run out of gas. They had gone on a hunting trip and ran out of gas a couple miles down the beach, so they asked if we could give them a ride back. We said, "Why don't you have a cup of coffee with us?" We made them some pancakes. So we're sitting there talking. I asked them what boat they were from. He says, "The ———" and it went just silent. It was the boat that had fired at us. And he knew who we were, so he didn't really want to say. We all just looked at each other. Then I said, "Well, what's your skipper like?" And he said, "Well, I know what happened. I really don't like the skipper that much but he's a good fisherman. That's why I fish for him, but a lot of the things he does I don't agree with." He shot at two little girls from California who didn't even know how to use guns. But now we do!

Rebecque: To explain the operation a little bit: we have two skiffs and then the jitney—that's about twenty-two feet. We travel by tying off the little skiff behind the big skiff and just towing it. So Laurie and I will drive the big skiff and then Don, the guy we fished with this year, drives the jitney. We move pretty slow 'cause we have so much gear. And the jitney sometimes has problems.

Laurie: Even if I explain how the whole thing works and draw pictures, it may not make sense. But to give a simple idea of beach seining: the jitney has a seine in it. He makes a set by taking off from the beach and laying the seine out. He'll go out straight at first, and he'll make a "U." To set the hook, he basically makes a "9." Then he'll open up the seine and pull hard, if the current is pulling the seine, or he'll just open it up again to let more fish in. But what he'll do is go back to the beach and so basically you'll have a "U" there. We'll have an anchor with a shoreline attached that holds the jitney onto the beach. And we haul the seine into the jitney. We use a block and a winch. We aren't pursing the fish [closing them up in the net]; beach seiners can't purse them. We bring our money bag [the bag of fish] up onto the beach. We have to pull our leads [the weighted line at the bottom of the net] onto the beach when we have our money bag. We bring most of the seine in by the winch and the block, haul it in that way.

Everyone thinks beach seining is so hard because we have to pull it through the block. But we have a snap and ring system. Or on the cork line [line of buoys] there's rings and there's a haul line that's snapped to it. And so he uses a winch to bring that in to get slack. Then we bring in that slack and then we lay the seine back into the jitney. Also a trick to that, to make sure you have enough slack so that fish can't dive under the leads, we bring up the leads, the cork, and the web; we bring all three in since we have three people.

Once we have the money bag, we attach the cork, tie the fish off to the skiff. Then we tighten the web so we have a little bag of fish and one of us will hop in the skiff and will brail [scoop] them out. The brailer [small net with a handle] is in the skiff. We do it by hand. That's a lot of fun. That's where it all pays off. It's a lot of work, but it's so fun having all these fish pour in on you.

Laurie: This year we've been catching a lot of fish. Our day-to-day schedule goes something like this. We try to get out on the beach between 10:00 A.M. and noon, which is pretty late, but sometimes we wouldn't get home until like 4:00 A.M. because of delivering the fish. We also like to take at least an hour in the morning drinking coffee, because when we're really catching fish, we don't even eat dinner. We eat ice cream for dinner. We eat peanut butter and jelly sandwiches all day. So in the morning we like to make a good breakfast, just be at peace with ourselves, make plans about what we're going to do, where we're going to go.

We put together a little lunch box, decide what beach we're going to go to. We decide that by the direction of the wind. There are beaches that are better at a certain tide. Our best beach is Flamingo Beach, but that gets some pretty heavy surf when it's blowing, so we can't always fish it.

The first couple of days we were in Spiridon Bay, but it wasn't very great. So we came down into Uyak Bay. We made a few sets and they weren't real great either. When we talked to this other beach seiner, he said they were killing them over in Spiridon. We laughed at ourselves—"We go where there's no fish." But the next day we started catching like 10,000 pounds a day, and that's pretty much what it's been all summer. It's just been great.

We work until it gets dark or if we make a water haul [no fish], then we'll watch for jumpers [salmon that jump out of the water]. If we start seeing jumpers again, we'll go ahead and make a set. And sometimes we'll move and go somewhere else. Because we know some beaches are not that great on that tide, we'll go to another that is better. We'll fish as long as we can, making set after set.

Don holds the hook [holds the net open] for about a half hour, and it takes about a half hour to pull it in, so it takes about an hour per set. Then there's time to load the fish in the skiff. That can be more challenging on the ebb, especially if there's surf, because you're trying to hold the skiff off while you're trying to brail the fish into the skiff, which seiners don't have to deal with. So that can be hard. We were fishing until about midnight, 1 A.M. We've made a couple of sets at night, when it was dark.

Rebecque: If you're fishing on a rocky beach, it's a lot harder. A clean beach definitely makes it more enjoyable. Otherwise if you're fishing where there's lot of rocks, the seine gets caught up on the rocks. If it's unprotected, the wind blows harder and the seine can collapse. We've been lucky at Flamingo Beach—there are no rocks there.

Last summer there was a time with the first guy we fished with when he was making a set and it was caught on a rock. Laurie and I were just coming to the beach with the skiff and were about to unload it and he yells, "Get me out of here! I got caught on a rock. We need to get this sucker back home quick!" We just dropped all our stuff and hopped out there and started backhauling the whole seine back into the jitney. He could have lost the whole seine from that one mistake.

Laurie: I would never fish for him again. If there was a rock or a reef, he would find it. This summer we haven't even had to backhaul once. Here's the first thing I remember happening in beach seining. The guy we were fishing with had an extension put on the davit [pole that holds the seine block], which the seine goes through. All of a sudden there's this loud noise. And I'm like, "What?" I see the block coming right at my face and it hit the davit and broke it. The block was swinging right in front of my face. I came this close to going out. That was really scary. This was the first week. And I'm thinking, "What am I doing out here?" But the fortunate thing was the guy at the cannery who fixed it for him told him to put another pipe inside [for sturdiness] just in case something happened, so that basically saved my life. I just felt like it was a test. I got past it, I accepted it. I understood that this was dangerous and that things could happen which made me more aware.

Rebecque: One time I was driving the big skiff towing the little skiff with a fuel drum in it and all of our gear and the dog. And we're going around Outlet Cape. The waves were pretty big—it was scary. And I've got both motors going, a thirty-five and a fifty-five horse, and I'm trying to get around and back in as quickly as possible. I knew that Don could take care of himself. I went around Outlet Cape and made it. Then I see Don and he's out in the waves, except his motor was only going in one direction. He could only turn circles. I thought, "God! I'm his crew member. I have to take care of him. I have to turn around and go back out there and see what is wrong." Even though I know he's like superman, he can do anything, it was my obligation to do that. I was so scared. I turned the skiff around and went all the way back out there and yelled, "Okay, what's going on?" He said, "It's all right.

It's just going in one direction. I'll just go in circles a few minutes here and it'll be okay." So I turned back around and went back in. So just doing that, doing what I had to do even though I was scared made me feel really good—"I can do it! I have to have confidence. I know I can do it." There are so many great things out here. There's freedom and the land and there's friendly people and good people to work with. You're feeling mentally and physically well because you know you can do the work.

3 "I Can't Work with This Woman!"

MAY 28, 1978, BEAR ISLAND, ALASKA

I am hopeful there will be no resistance to my fishing with the men, either from the men or the women. I am not sure. I don't know if Duncan has told them yet. We decided shortly after we were engaged. It wasn't a big decision; it seemed the most natural thing to do, that we would share the work. But only the men fish in this family. I do not want to be shut up in the house, though the women work just about as hard, it seems to me. No one except Duncan is greeting my presence in the skiff with joy.

*M*y journals tell no dramatic stories of harassment and discrimination, just the quiet story of pushing against family tradition to be the first woman to work in the skiff. My narrative is tame, and even my most difficult memories come from being treated equally. There were no excuses for staying ashore: fatigue, a hurting back, a cold, cramps . . . The brothers each worked through their own assortment of ills and maladies, from numb arms and carpal tunnel syndrome to flu and strained shoulders, and I was expected to do the same. And at first I did, without complaint, almost. It was a test, and I've always been good at tests. If I passed, I would earn and prove my worth in the skiff. I don't know exactly when it happened, but I slowly came to realize that equality was treacherous and unfair. The men all weighed at least sixty pounds more than me; I simply did not have their body weight or muscle mass to torque to my advantage. And when the wind was blowing forty and we were out in it and I alone had to hold the net to keep our skiff from splintering against the reefs, there was no room or time for size and weight deliberations, for calculating what amount of work was fair for each body mass. Paradoxically, it was the lack of discrimination that weighed most on me. Other working wives tell the same story.

That equality and complete inclusion for me eventually seemed a kind of reverse discrimination. But you won't hear this complaint from the women in this chapter. Each asked only for equal treatment and equal opportunity. That doesn't come automatically in a job where you need the strength to land a swinging 130-pound crab pot, the endurance to withstand thirty-six straight hours of work without sleep, the moxie to run a 150-horsepowered seine skiff at full speed near reefs, and special hands-on skills like diesel engine repair and maintenance, net-mending, operating hydraulics. These are the powers that win the day and the fish; these are the powers fishing women must prove to disbelieving men. And not least of all, there is active resistance from an unexpected quarter—other women, the wives of the men who fish. You will hear this also.

But this chapter as well is about a set of hurdles set not by families but by larger traditions, traditions we almost can't articulate but somehow all know. This set begins with the ocean itself. Although since ancient times and across many cultures the sea has been female, women on the sea have occupied limited spaces. They have clung to bowsprits, their carved, angular breasts breaking ocean into wake; their faces have gone to sea on men's tattooed arms;

their names have labeled the bows and sterns of men's boats. But few have themselves ridden the waves and worked the boats that sail them.

In this man's world fishing women greet harassment and discrimination every day with little hope of recourse but their determination and their skills. The elaborate code devised by Congress to define and enforce sexual harassment laws may work on land, but they don't take well to water. A fishing vessel is its own family, its own country, and the skipper is father, president, and often dictator, no matter how small or large the boat. The conflict takes many forms, from the "two-for-one" syndrome when a skipper hires a woman as cook and expects her to double as bunkmate, though she may not know it, to obscenities and verbal barrages attacking competency to life-threatening attacks.

But you must know that not every woman who fishes experiences resistance. Those who enter through family or other personal relationships oftentimes are encouraged in their work and sheltered. Even some women who have made their way alone have nothing but good things to say of the men with whom they have worked. The four stories in this chapter have not been chosen because they represent the most extreme and dramatic examples of discrimination. Though Virginia Adams's story certainly is dramatic and extreme, I have heard other stories from friends of friends (most of whom no longer live in Alaska) that suggest more brutal treatment nearing slavery. Yet I chose not to hunt these stories down. However true or false they are, and I could not know which, they are so far from the realm of most women's experiences that nothing is to be gained from the sensationalism. The remaining stories then are somewhere in the middle, between those who have known little resistance and those who cite a career of resistance. And as such, they speak for many.

Virginia Adams

Virginia met with considerable resistance to getting hired in Alaska. Even after she proved she wasn't a "greenie," men still harassed her as she worked on one boat while her husband, Jon, worked on another.

It was hard to get a job at first in Alaska. I had no luck at all. Jon got a job as a skiff man on a seiner. I pounded the docks and got the typical—I could go for half share and be really sweet with the captain. I already had seven years of commercial fishing under the belt but no one knew me, so that didn't carry any weight. I did get some work mending seine. I was pretty discouraged because it took a while in New York to get established as a commercial fisherman. It got to the point where I had a really good relationship with the other fishermen there. It was all behind me, the breaking the ice. Then I came here and had to do it all over again.

I'll never forget the psych I would have had to give myself to walk down the dock in Kodiak and ask for a job. I don't know how old I was—early twenties—and nothing but this continuous sizing me up and whistles and would I do this and . . . You have to have nerves of steel to go through it, and I'd just take a breath after each time. They'd say, "Yeah, you can come on if you'll ———." You just roll your eyes, turn around, walk away, realize that person's a jerk, and hopefully things will work out. There were days I told Jon, "Forget it, I'm going home. I'm not going to go through this." I would look at these jerks on deck who could hardly sew a three bar [mend a small hole in the net] and I knew I had so much experience and they're talking to me like this . . . I just felt like I could do some terrible things. But I didn't because I really wanted to maintain this good first impression in the fleet. I couldn't flip off some captain or swear back—I had to be above reproach.

And that's the thing about being a woman in fishing. You have to be twice as good. You've really got to have good skills and keep your mouth shut for a while. It's a lot easier said than done. During times of harassment—as long as it's not serious harassment, someone's not threatening you—you've got to kind of take it. There's no recourse in this industry.

There are other problems working on a boat, especially as a woman. Everybody's looking for you to slip up, assumes you're going to be sleeping with everyone's husband. It's discouraging to have to fight that as well as do your work. And I'll tell you, the biggest problem is the wives. Boy the trouble I've had on that front has been incredible at times! The captain's wife is convinced you're a sweet young thing. Maybe their husband's a great guy, but you're going to lure him away. But women are so suspicious of each other, you know. And I don't blame women. I have the same, when my husband Jon's been joint venture fishing and they hire women—I'm always checking her out. Especially when you know your husband's going to be at sea for six months. This is all human nature.

When I got started seining, I'll never forget going up to the flying bridge and asking the captain, "Would you like a cup of coffee?" I feel most crew should extend that to a captain who's up there driving the boat in the weather—it had nothing to do with my sex. He's captain, I'm crew.

He said, "Yeah, Virginia, that would be great." Then the other guy said, "Yeah, and I take such and such in mine." And I said, "Well you can get yours yourself."

I know it was terrible, but right away I had to do this or I was going to be put in this role. And the captain was being so gentlemanly with me, which I knew wasn't going to cut it either.

On one boat I had a little bit of trouble. Not with the captain at all. The captain and I got along really well, but we ran through quite a few guys who couldn't seem to handle me being a woman. I was given this job to sort of take control of the deck and everything and that's what I did. And there's some people that have a hard time with it. They'd say, "I can't work with this woman anymore!" The captain would say, "Fine, you won't be working with that woman. We'll find somebody else." They all got their walking papers. And that was the other thing. It was intimidating for them to be around somebody who quite obviously had more skill than they did. So I would be trying to teach them how to do something efficiently, and just some guys, I don't care if you're more experienced than they are or not, they can't handle it. I came up with a couple of them in a row and I got disgusted. I eventually left.

When we were cod fishing, there was one guy who really tried to get me in trouble. And I could have lost my life on that one. That was on the *Predator,* a sixty-two-foot boat. And I was first mate on there and I had just broken in a fellow who was great to work with. He was actually a good friend of mine. And I was looking to get off the boat. So I told the captain, "I'm going to be getting off the boat soon. Why don't we try to find another guy that I can break in on a couple of trips before I go so he knows what's going on?" The one fellow was already up to speed and really a great hand. So we took this other fellow along.

It was apparent to me right from the get-go he wasn't going to be any good. For one thing he couldn't tolerate me at all. He couldn't take any direct order from me without telling me a better way to do it, or blah, blah, blah . . . I immediately told the captain, "This guy has got a real problem with me and it's probably not going to work out." "Let's give it a trip," the captain said. A trip's about four days. So I showed the guy how to set up the gill net for set-out (putting the nets in the water). You know, we had all the anchors, flag buoys set out against the rail. Set-out with those gill nets was fast. You didn't want to do anything wrong or get in the way of anything 'cause you could go overboard.

Well, this guy at this point hated me. We went to setting out this string of gill nets, and I had explained to these guys exactly how to do everything. There's a particular way to set it up. And there's a particular thing you never do, which I had explained to him a hundred times. And so, what does he do? The very thing I told him not to! He picks up the anchor forward of me on the boat and he walks at me with it in his hand and he has it on the inside of the boat. You never do it! You just pick the anchor up and throw it off the rail and the lines are all on the outside so you never come inside of the boat with it. Well, he gets between me and the stern of the boat with the anchor and I'm going to go overboard with it. There is no doubt, and it's going to happen fast. The other guy saw what was happening and he screamed, he was screaming at the top of his lungs at the captain, "Reverse! Reverse!" 'cause he knows I'm going to go in the water. So I threw myself into the stays [supports] that go up into the boat. There's usually chain and a cable there. So I got myself onto this chain, so when the anchor hit me I wouldn't go over. And then the anchor just came and hooked me right in the back. The only thing keeping me from flying off the stern is the chain stay on the boom. And the whole time I'm just looking at this guy saying, "If I get out of this, you're dead, you're just dead!"

Well, I got out of it because with the guy screaming reverse, the captain just put it full bore in reverse. I was so relieved that I wasn't going over. Matter of fact, what happened was the other crewman became unglued and went at the guy. The captain came down and broke it up; so I didn't have to get so involved. And the captain told him to go down to his bunk and just stay there. And then the guy went off and said, "I can't be working with that woman." And the captain said, "You're not going to be working with that woman, you're outta here!" That was really a bad situation. And that fellow went on to throw a man overboard, offshore, off a dragger and ended up doing a prison term for it.

Things haven't really changed. Fishing for women is not for the weak of heart. By nature of the occupation and the people involved, you're going to come up against some very crude people. You know, shockingly so. And if that stuff curls your hair, you have to be well prepared for men to be extremely disgustingly, explicit sexually with you. It's power. They want to embarrass you. I used to be very hotheaded, angry about it. Now I just kind of laugh. When I got started I was intimidated, I didn't have eighteen years of fishing behind me. You know, first I got angry and would want to get angry, then as I matured I would ignore those guys as much as possible. Now it happens less and less to me. It doesn't really happen at all anymore. Maybe because I'm older or maybe I just haven't come across those kind of men anymore.

Lisa Jakubowski

I first met Lisa when she hired on at a fish camp down the beach from us. It was blowing; the surf on their beach was too high to get the skiff ashore, so she and her skipper had come to our more protected island to wait out the storm. I was curious about her. It was unusual for a woman to be hired on as full-time crew in our kind of fishing, but she was clearly more than competent. She started in 1984, beating the docks for a job on a fishing boat. In the following years she worked at longlining, setnetting, and seining.

The year '89 started out horribly but ended up on a good note. I was getting discouraged by the harassment. The working and living conditions were miserable. I slept in the foc'sle. You've got four bunks, two on each side, two high. Usually I was the only woman. A lot of times the crew would be interested in getting to know me more on an intimate level. I remember this one guy who wanted to have heart-to-heart talks with me every night before we went to sleep. He'd say, "You should pay more attention to me." It's like I had to make sure everybody was happy. It seemed as though they liked me, but if I didn't fall in love with them they'd turn on me and hate me and make my life miserable.

When I quit out in Dutch Harbor in '89, two other guys quit with me. We had to wait a few days for the ferry. This one guy was following me around drunk. And there's this little catwalk where you go over some water. He was pretending like he was falling. I pulled him back up on the catwalk and I was so mad at him I slapped him really hard and told him to leave me alone. When he got back to the room, I heard that the hand mark was still on his face. That was the one who wanted to have heart-to-heart talks. Stories are still being told. One time he was down there and he was drunk. The skipper heard this. He heard him say, "Lisa, I love you! I love you!" I don't remember this but the skipper remembers hearing me yell back, "Shut up!"

Another guy on the boat just had it out for me for some reason. He'd do things like put chickens on my pillow, put a chicken in my bunk, just irritating little things. There are a lot of practical jokes that go on, but they knew it wasn't wanted. After months and months of this I just felt like "Get away! Give me my space!"

And then there was another guy on another boat who at first seemed really nice and attentive, overly attentive. I just wanted to work and be friends and then he just turned 180 degrees and made my life miserable. In fact, he was the reason I had to leave the boat. It was extreme harassment—verbal more so than physical—but it's just as effective, probably more so.

I was long-lining out of Kodiak on a catcher-processor. I was hired as deckhand. I was the only woman. It started off the minute I got on board. First of all it was in fun—"Oh my god it's a woman!" I got on the boat and they said they'd "give me a try." That was not encouraging. I knew within the first day this was going to be the hardest job. I was going to have to deal with putting up with these four guys and the skipper. They thought it was so odd for a woman to be on there. They made me realize constantly that I was not one of them, I was something different. I just wanted to make money. I had just bought a house down in Washington and needed to make mortgage payments.

We started out doing boat maintenance. We were supposed to go out for gray cod, but breakdowns and bad weather kept us in. So we finally got all the bugs worked out the first week of February and went out. We made a halfway decent trip, but I couldn't stand it any longer. Everything was fine for the first couple of months, but then I got the feeling this certain person disliked me. He was a fellow deckhand, supposedly, but in his mind he was the deck boss. Anytime I tried to make a decision, he'd come by and make the opposite decision. So I just kind of stepped back and waited for him to tell me what to do. Ended up I had to stand, working next to him while he was yelling at the top of his lungs obscene words like "bitch, cunt, whore." He's not calling me this directly; there's lots of music going on. He was just "expressing himself," but I knew it was a power trip. I just tried to take it because I couldn't do anything else. The skipper was just as bad. He wouldn't tell them to stop. I was in this position where I had to prove myself and pull my weight. But it seemed the harder I worked, the more he hated me. I don't know. I believe he had a cocaine problem and an alcohol problem. How can you figure those people out? So I finally quit. As soon as the boat got into town I left. When I left I didn't want to leave. I was in tears because I didn't know what I was going to do.

I felt like the whole time I should not have to be putting up with these work conditions. And I called the State Department of Human Resources. I just wanted to know the definition of sexual harassment. And they said "any working condition that's hostile." Well, that was definitely hostile. It definitely was the reason for my leaving. But to report it I would need documentation and witnesses. There's no way! I think the woman I spoke to had had some reports from processors. But this is a fishing boat; it's independent. You're out there on your own. That was a real low point in my career.

If I were a man getting on a boat, they would see me as a worker instead of how they see me now, which is "Oh my god it's a woman!" I was painting yesterday on the *Enterprise* and this guy I worked with last year was on a boat across the way. He had a couple of young guys on there and they go, "Whoa, look at that woman over there!" This guy I work with goes, "Yeah and she can work too." I guess it shut them up. I don't understand what they mean when they say that. Do they think they're the only ones who can work? Or the only ones who have the right to the ocean? Or to physical labor? I don't know what the deal is.

I worked in the forest service before I came up here. I was on a fire crew. There were women toting chain saws and stuff, and some of the guys couldn't because they had to get certified. I was used to that. Then when I worked on the processor, they kept all the women cleaning the galley while the guys are out on deck. Oh I got hot! I got pissed! I wanted to learn something new and I let them know it. "I'm not here to clean!" I did get to go on deck once they knew. They said, "Oh, we always thought the women wanted to stay inside." Well, not me.

Yeah, this fishing industry's just bizarre. I don't think it's changed much in the twelve years I've been fishing. There are more women on the docks than ten years ago, but there are still these guys that think the women are strange objects on board.

Being a woman makes it much more difficult to get on those little salmon boats. When I walk the docks looking for salmon jobs, I'd get things like, "Yeah, I'd like to hire you, but you know how it is." The skipper means his wife wouldn't let him. I remember a bunch of guys once saying, "Yeah, we need someone but not you! Ha! Ha!" I'd just leave saying to them, "Your loss!" "My loss too," I'd say under my breath. I had one guy tell me I was too good looking. I thought, "If I shave my head will you hire me then?"

And also the living conditions make it hard. The quarters are so small. I can understand how some guys wouldn't want to deal with it. But I used to be young and very immodest. Used to be. Not any more. I have my own stateroom now. And I'm not giving it up. When walking the docks, even now, I can't wear shirts that when I bend over are going to hang down, nothing too revealing. I'm constantly worrying about how I'm looking because I know eyes are on me.

It's very lonely being the only woman on a boat. I make a point of never getting involved with guys on a romantic level or anything. Friends, I'm always open to friends, but you always have to be careful that they don't think it's more. See, there are so many different levels of guys. I don't want to be friends with the drunkards and cocaine addicts. But definitely the more respectable people I became friends with. And I have maintained male friendships and female friendships. There's a lot of loneliness though. I found out that laugh therapy helps. I go out on the back deck and just laugh to myself and feel better.

Last summer I saw a lot of young women coming here to fish. I encourage them—Go for it! I tell them, "Don't let their bullshit stop you. Just go do whatever you want. But just be prepared to fight if you need to, or put up with things. Just be aware it's difficult." I remember one girl a few years ago, a real thin pretty girl. She came back from walking the docks all upset because some guys told her to go put on some weight and come back and ask. And she was so upset. And I told her, "Look, this is the way it is. You can't change it." But actually you can, I think. The more women that fish, the more it'll change. Yeah, they do need someone strong, but they also need someone who's going to be there, who's not going to be in the bar drinking or in jail for cocaine. It's so easy for guys to come up and make money if they're a little bit intelligent, can work hard, are dependable. For a woman to do it, it's a little more difficult. But it's never been just brute strength. I've been able to work longer and harder than some of the guys I've worked with because I have a pig-headed attitude. I wanted to work. You get a guy on there who doesn't want to work, he's not going to. You can't just say, male versus female in how much energy they're going to put out. In a lot of ways, it's more a matter of energy and technique than strength. There were definitely instances where I would have wished I had a little more muscle power, but I think it's more know-how.

There are so many different reasons a woman is hired on board. I've been hired not so much as a worker, but as wanting to get to know me—an intimate relationship, but when working, I don't think of that as acceptable. I'd rather be hired as someone to do the work.

Christine Holmes

Christine worked in numerous fisheries for more than ten years. She was diagnosed with breast cancer shortly after our interview and fought the disease with the same intensity that made her so successful as a fishing woman. After a two-year struggle she died in May 1996. Christine was always quick to defend fishermen and considered her treatment fair with one major exception—the "John Wayne" skipper she confronted in the Bering Sea.

I wouldn't say I was necessarily discriminated against or sexually harassed in my fishing career. All my friends pretty much fish and a lot of guys my age who have been fishing as long as I have have been through the same stuff I've been through. It's just part of fishing. You pay your dues. It's the rite of passage. I feel like this job I have now, I went through my college, my graduate, and my post-graduate and now I'm on a good boat. Now I might make six figures this year, if the fish prices are good. I might not. And sure I've been hazed. I mean, I can remember the old wheelwatch, no—anchor watch. This guy said, "You're going to have to watch the anchor." So I sat out there on deck for an hour watching the anchor. I actually thought this was something you had to do. I had no idea! I've seen myself do the same kind of things to people who don't know about fishing. It's just something fishermen do. We like to tease people.

I get such a kick out of this guy at Western Cannery. He's probably the world's oldest dock attendant. Really cute little guy, probably right near retirement age. Well, our boat ties up and he says, "What are you doing on the boat? Are you the skipper's wife?" I said, "No, I'm a deckhand." He said, "Aww, all you gals trying to pull my leg." First I was the skipper's wife. Then I was the girlfriend of one of the guys on the boat. Then I was the cook. He wouldn't let his eyes tell him the truth. After about three or four times on the boat coming in, I was down helping Jerry weld one day, he goes, "You really are a deckhand aren't you?" I go, "Yes, I am."

If you want to get me going, ask me if I'm the cook on the boat. If someone asks me, I just smile and say, "No, I'm a deckhand." I'm usually a really nice person. Sometimes they go, "Yeah, right, you're a deckhand." I say, "Come down and watch me work." Or I'll ask them, "Can you splice cable?" And they go, "No." "Does your cook splice cable?" "No." "Well I must not be the cook then." I like to get them going. Sometimes they'll be working and can't find a bit or something. I always have bits with me; I have my little tools I carry around with me. The guys say, "God, you're so cool, Christy."

Now I'm dragging on the *Hazel Rene*, which is a 140-foot dragger, and that's what I've always wanted to do—dragging. I've done a lot of other fisheries besides that. I went up to work on a factory boat originally this season. I was promised work as an assistant cook. They said that once the skipper found out I had all this knowledge of nets—I've gone to trawl school and everything—that he would put me right on deck, which was where I wanted to be. I've always worked as a deckhand. Well, it didn't turn out that way at all. They didn't have a contract for me. And I said, "I'd really like to sign a contract before I get on the boat." Well, they said they hadn't set them up yet and that the boat was leaving. I got on the boat and found out I would be cooking for thirty-four people. And they called the morning before I left Cordova and said, "Oh, by the way, did we tell you you would have to process, too? But only when there's a lot of fish."

I got up there and I was cooking eight hours a day, which was no problem, but then this personnel woman said, "You know, we're really being pushed by the labor board. We've got to hire women, but the guys won't go for it. So we'll send you out as assistant cook, but once they find out you've had all this experience, they'll put you on deck. We'll say you're an assistant cook, but we really need to have a woman on deck." Apparently they had a lot of women apply for deckwork, but none of them had experience until I showed up.

It was just nuts. The skipper told me, "Well gal," just like John Wayne, "if you can do all your other work, you're welcome to work on deck with the guys in your spare time." So I did. I worked sixteen-hour days. Every chance I had I got out on deck. Sometimes I worked twenty-hour days. On coffee break I'd go do my cooking. I was wearing this poor skipper down, 'cause I just wasn't going to give up. I walked in the wheelhouse one day to overhear him say to one of the deckhands, "Oh that little gal from Cordova has a lot to learn. She's going to find out it's a heck of a lot different up here in the Bering Sea than it is working on some little gill net down there in a nice warm warehouse in Cordova." And I said, "Oh really?" It was just hysterical. And I said, "You know, I've been fishing for ten years and I really haven't had to deal with any discrimination until now. You know, what's the furthest you've ever fished offshore?" He said, "Oh, 170, 200 miles." I said, "Well, try 1,500. You'd be amazed but I really do know what's going on." It was just ridiculous.

We finished the elephant sole season and they still didn't have a contract for me. Most of the employees were Mexicans with green cards but they all had contracts. But I still had not seen one, so of the three boats this company has, they let all the crew go except for about ten people. They kept me because they needed their nets rebuilt. I'm good enough to rebuild the nets but I'm not good enough to work on deck. I had just about had it but I didn't want to quit because I knew that in Dutch Harbor it's so hard to find jobs. You know you should never go there unless you have a job. So I thought I'll just look for another job. I'll stay with this and keep the money coming in but look elsewhere.

I had been there in Dutch Harbor already for three months and I couldn't find another job. And I thought, "I've fished for eleven years. I've been through some hard times, but I can't get a job up here—it's like the old boys' club." I was walking down by Petro Marine in Dutch Harbor. A cab came hurtling toward me and hit a mud puddle and covered me in mud. And I said, "That's it. I'm going home. I can't do this anymore." And it was that evening I ran into Jerry and Nonny and they hired me on the *Hazel Rene*.

See, a lot of guys are worried about discrimination suits now. And that makes it harder for me to get a job. You'd think the feminist movement would make things easier. It's really scared a lot of guys. I think these are difficult times for men because roles have changed so much. They don't know where they stand anymore. It's not their fault; it's just society's changing so much.

There have been problems with women observers out on the big boats saying, "Oh, I've been discriminated against for sexual harassment." It hasn't improved things at all for women getting jobs because the poor guys are so paranoid. And I see observers out there getting real frisky with these guys on board. And I've said, "Hey, I've fished for a long time. You don't see me running around." You just don't do it.

What's that old saying, "Don't shake the tree if you don't want the peaches"? A boat is not a place to flirt with a bunch of guys. And I think you have to deal with it professionally. I think it would be really wise for men in these observer companies to maybe make that part of their training, you know, handle yourself as a professional on a boat. A lot of these kids are so young, they're right out of college. I hate to say it, but it does make it difficult for those of us that do fish. I had one girl tell me, "I've been fishing all my life. What makes you so special?" I said, "Well, I haven't slept with everyone I fished with." That's what sets me apart. If I have a daughter someday I want her to be able to fish. I don't want her to be an object, but a lot of it is the women themselves making things difficult.

I've talked to a couple of women in Dutch Harbor who were asking how I got into fishing. You have to have a good sense of humor. You can't take bullshit too seriously. I'm a really sensitive person who at times suffers from extremely low self-esteem and I still manage to do it. But I think a lot of gals think the world is going to change just because they're a woman who wants to fish. I think that's asking a lot. This has been a male thing for a long time. I'm Norwegian. The Vikings fished, a lot of the native women fished. But don't go in expecting these guys to change overnight. Go in and have a good sense of humor, do the best you can do, keep your boots dry, pay attention, the rest will come easy. But I see women show up on a boat and the first thing they'll do is go into the head and take all the *Playboy*s and throw them away. I really don't think that's my place or their place. You don't have to look at the stuff. You've got to give a little bit, not be too much of a feminist. What's important is being a team player, working hard, and getting the fish in. You're out there to fish. The rest of the stuff . . . I don't know if I'm explaining it.

And also I think too that women that go to a boat and say the guy says, "Gee I'd really like to hire you, but I just got married last year. My wife would go nuts if I had a woman on the boat." There are lots of boats out here where the guy isn't married or where there isn't a problem with it. I for one can understand the jealousy of a wife with a guy out fishing. Especially if it's a guy and a gal out. I've been in that situation where I was with a man for three years and he said, "How do you feel about my taking a gal out on the boat?" I said, "I'm not really impressed with the one you want to take, but I'd be the last person, with my position in fishing, to say no." I went down to the boat and caught him in bed with her. This has a tendency to really piss a person off. I can understand how the wife feels. Someday if I get married and I have a boat with somebody, yeah I would hire women, but I'm not sure I would say, "Sure Hon, hire a whole bunch of gals and go fishing."

That's one thing—I feel like I've had to sacrifice some things for fishing. There are men who are real threatened by me. One guy, we were together for three years. Every time he would go fishing when I was with him, it would be a problem. When I tendered with him, he was very jealous. He was sure I was up to no good. Actually it was a very abusive relationship. Hopefully other women don't have to go through that kind of abuse, but a lot of guys don't understand a woman who wants to fish. I think there must be some men who do. I often thought I should move to Kodiak. Maybe guys are a little more accepting up there. They're real threatened by it here, and it's too bad because I think if you talk with guys who fish with their wives—they're an asset. There is something about having a woman on the boat. I'll go up and bring a cup of coffee and talk to them about their kids and stuff the guys don't normally do. It's too bad most men are so threatened by women. I think, too, it's a real insecurity that makes them like that.

There are some boats I don't even approach. I get a feeling. I can always tell by looking at the guys. You just see the way they walk across the deck and I know if I go on and say, "Do you have a boat job?" And the guys say, "Yeah, gal, I've got a job for you." I can see those guys, I almost can feel what they are. So I don't even go to those boats anymore. But that's from ten, eleven years of experience. I can remember, god, just the first couple of years I fished going home, being almost in tears because these guys had this real cocky attitude. I would just feel so dumb, but that's part of it. I'm not saying it's right, but you can't expect things to change overnight. I think eventually with more women like myself and Riki Ott and other gals fishing, it'll change. I mean you can have all the laws you want to, but it isn't going to help women get hired more on boats.

Laurie Knapp

Laurie Knapp is married, has two young daughters, shops at Safeway, and tells calmly of being blown off an exploding boat into the ocean, hair melted to her head. That happened when she was seventeen, the year she left Minnesota to come to Alaska. That was the start of a fifteen-year fishing career that has taken her from the Bering Sea all the way to Mexico. Eight of those years were spent in the Bering Sea during the boom years of the king crab fishery. While she didn't experience harassment, she had to overcome less-than-subtle resistance to her presence.

While out crabbing, I didn't initially do a lot of deck work. I went on as cook and I would come out on deck and just watch and stay out of the way. A lot of boats that I shipped out on didn't accept women on deck at all. In fact one boat I went out on, I ran to help bring a pot over the rail and somebody screamed at the top of his lungs, "Look out!" I thought, "My god, is there a boom falling?" Then he yelled again, "There's a woman at the rail!" Look out—a woman!

It's a very macho environment where they don't want to accept women because it's their deal. I knew enough about crab fishing at that point, bringing a pot aboard when it's flat calm isn't that big of a deal. I just slowly worked into it—got out and filled bait jars and then slowly, somebody's off doing something else, and I'd fill in: help with the coiling, do a little bit of this, of that. Then gradually I was on deck working the hydraulics, bringing freight on board. They see you can handle a little bit more and then they'll allow you a little more freedom. Being a woman, you have to slowly work into that kind of position. Be very passive and submissive, and I learned that growing up. I grew up in that kind of society, so I knew how to do that.

Later, after I fished with Steve, my ex-husband, I tendered on the *Ironhead.* That was my first job ever as total deck person, not a cook— Peggy Smith was the cook—and this was tendering out in Bristol Bay. And that was a fun job. I really enjoyed having another woman on board and not being the cook for once so I could concentrate totally on running the hydraulics, two cranes, running them at once, taking salmon on board, and doing everything. Wheelwatches, using all the electronics, navigating, all this stuff was really a thrill.

But there was resistance from some of the fishermen. When they would see that I was the person who was running the hydraulics and bringing these bags of fish out of their gill net boat onto the tender, I had several skippers say, "I don't want her running the hydraulics." And I would walk right up to them and say, "Well then, go to a different tender." And they'd be taken aback. I mean they really expect women to be passive and not speak their mind. But they didn't have a choice. As soon as they could see that I wasn't crashing bags into their rigging and that I was very careful and fast, then there was no problem.

Generally speaking the men scared me. Not so much as a fear of them, but they were so boisterous, so male, running around on deck, shooting at sea lions, trying to kill anything that was alive. I didn't really like a lot of that stuff that went on. They get so bored, I think, out there and just find anything to give them a little bit of humor.

I fished on the *Retriever* one spring with Kim Tippett, and Pam Hom was on the *Husky* with Dave Tippett; Peggy was fishing on the *Airedale,* boats all owned by Harold Daupenspeck. So in the yard down in Seattle in Lake Washington, before the season would begin, all us women, we'd be down there together, and that's when I really began to know a lot more women. We'd work in the yard together to get the boats ready to go fishing. That's when I started to form partnerships, at least talking on the radio with other women, telling stories, getting together with other women. For a while there I was totally alone, it seemed like. Slowly we began to form almost a club.

The summer Peggy and I were on the *Ironhead* together, that's when I decided I always want to be on a boat with a woman or to have some balance of the sexes. That way you're not overpowered so much by all the male dominance of "This is your job, you stick to it." And even conversations can become very male oriented—hunting, killing, they get very basic—but with another woman on board there's more talk about arts or literature or something. The summer with Peggy really bonded us together; we've been good friends—we live across the street from each other now and we both have children. We fished with Mary Jacobs on the *Renaissance* together, and all us women got pregnant at the same time. We all went fishing together that summer and we all got pregnant. A few men actually asked how that happened with an all-woman crew.

I much prefer working with other women. Fishing with Mary Jacobs, with an all-woman crew, was a real high for me. I loved working with women because we ate whatever whenever we wanted to. If it was cottage cheese and peas, it was fine. It wasn't—"Where's the meat?" And we were in the top 10 percent of the money makers in the seining fishery. It's not like we were struggling out there—inept, weak women. I mean, we're doing good, we're fishing off the capes, and really push, push, push! Mary is a damn good fisherman, and I felt real proud to work with her. It was great being able to travel across the Shelikof, no other boats around, and all of us in the sun, taking our shirts off and sitting up there on the flying bridge and just going, "This is just so wonderful!" And "Oh, I'll do that! Let me do that!" With a man, you always did all the low jobs, the dishes, cleaning out the holds. It's hard to get men to work as hard as women do. And I'm sorry to say that, all you men out in the world, but it's true. And to have a woman fight you to say, "Oh no, you go cook, I'll clean out the hold today, it's my turn." There was much more cooperation, much more sensitivity with women, much more laughter and fun. And I'm sure men have that too, you know, laughter and fun with themselves, but I don't believe they have the sensitivity and the caring and the mothering sort of friendships that women foster.

On the sexual side of things, I've never been close to being raped. Yes, I've had people approach me, from meek, mild skipper saying, "Gee, would you like to go to bed with me?" "Well, no, thanks," all the way to guys grabbing me. I was in a bar in Naknek and this little native was following me around—this is the most sexual pressure I've had—and he kept following me around and he was real cute and sweet and kept showing me pictures of his twelve kids and this and that. He was drinking and I was up ordering some beers for our table at the Red Dog Saloon and I felt his hand come up around my butt and I just turned around and hit. I wasn't even thinking, and he's real short, and I got him in the face and knocked him cold. I felt bad, but that's the way it goes. And he didn't bother me anymore. He was too drunk. It wasn't really my hit that knocked him out, he was really drunk. So that's the worst it ever got.

On the boats, there were times I locked myself in my stateroom because the guys wanted to party, party and I didn't want any part of it. It was too inane, gone on too long. But most of the boats I got on, these guys had mothers and sisters and basically respected women. There were times I felt totally alone, that I wasn't anything to them except to serve their next meal. And I could handle that.

The more women that are visible, the more it's just accepted with the younger fishermen. I'm sure there's still a lot of hesitancy with the older fishermen. I can remember pulling up alongside the *Miss Linda* and Jane, our skiffman, wasn't even able to use the bathroom because women were not allowed on board. She took the skiff over to his boat to get fuel and she had to pee and he wouldn't allow her inside the house to go to the bathroom, so she had to cross her legs and wait for us to pull up alongside.

So yeah, there's a lot of resistance still, I think. You probably don't hear about it so much anymore because there's more women running their own boats and crewmen and wives that want to do this now and daughters. It's becoming a lot more accepted.

4 *"When I Got My Own Boat . . ."*

JULY 15, 1993, UYAK BAY

Tami [my niece] and I went out in the skiff for the last pick together, our first time just the two of us. It was a perfect evening again, calm waters, little wind, even sunshine. As we worked together, side by side, I marveled over the arrangement. Yesterday she was a little girl, prissy, fearful, who came out in the skiff for short periods. I was always glad when she came out in Duncan's and my skiff: I wanted her to see that women could fish too, not just the men, that women were capable.

I felt proud to be running my own skiff again today. When all six skiffs rounded up and raced to the tender, I was second. While pitching fish, I felt like I belonged here. I have done this so many times before. I felt comfortable, that I had earned my place here in the lineup the hard way. That though I had babies at home, I could be here also.

*I*n the summer of 1979 a mysterious boat anchored up near our island. I passed it in the skiff on the way back from the tender one evening. It was tiny, not much larger than our own skiffs, with a minuscule makeshift cabin on it. And in a fleet of grays and blues and whites, this had a raven and a killer whale painted on it in bold strokes of black, red, and yellow. On the stern the incongruous name—The Invader. I almost laughed at the cheek and guts of it, that a boat this size, the smallest I had ever seen or heard of in the seining fleet, should go about so flagrantly, even suggesting by its name that it was some kind of force to be reckoned with.

As it turned out, the name and paint job were more than fitting. I found out later that week that not only did a full crew of four live and fish on that vessel but that the four were all women, even the skipper, Mary Jacobs. And I also found out that they were catching a lot of fish. Working as I did with all men, and seeing only men on the larger boats that passed by, it was wondrous to me. I marveled that they were strong enough to do the work by themselves, that they dared the blows and seas in that tiny boat, that they weren't intimidated by the men and their steel state-of-the-art vessels. Most of all, I wondered what it would be like to fish with all women.

I knew of and saw women in other fishing operations like ours who fished as I did, but my daily reality out on the water was as one woman working with five men. Gender didn't seem terribly relevant most of the time, except in certain occasions, like when one of us had to go to the bathroom. The bathroom in these cases was a quick drop-off to the nearest beach for me and over the side of the skiff for them. Either way, it introduced a new sense of privacy to the skiff and was a subtle reminder that under the uniform rain gear we all wore, we really were different.

Most of the lines that were drawn, though, had to do with experience. Because I had none, I was automatically crew, and Duncan skipper. It takes only two for a hierarchy, I found, but there was no resentment on my part. How could I dispute with someone who had been doing this work for twenty years? So when Duncan said, "Grab that line" or "Coil that running line tighter" or "You're putting the corks over the wrong way," I was smart enough to do what I was told. It's the maritime way. Not only that, but "too many cooks . . . ," "too many chiefs . . . ," and other clichés lent weight to this traditional arrangement. Later, as I caught on and gained skills and experience, I could anticipate much of what needed to be done; the orders came less often.

Eventually I began to run the outboard and later ran the skiff some of the time. Not with Duncan, but with hired crew. A single shift in position, from standing in the bow of the skiff to standing in the stern, bestowed the right to run the kicker and issue commands. I soon found, though, that the bow position, though it entailed more grunt work, was far easier than skippering even a "ship" the size of ours—a mere lollipop at twenty feet. The decisions, still, are many. Let me illustrate.

A few years ago, a crewman in his second year of fishing and I, in my twelfth, headed down to the nets for the morning pick of fish. The others were off on nets scattered in various other areas. It was blowing southwest and a nasty swell was cruising in from the Shelikof Strait already. We knew the forecast was for winds from the southwest at forty miles per hour, but we had no idea it was already this rough. I was running the kicker and was skipper for the day. As we bucked and surfed the four miles down to the nets, my stomach knotted tighter and tighter. It was all on me, whether we go or stay, whether we fight the rising wind and the swells and get the nets picked or turn around and head for safety. I should have done the latter. But I was responsible for getting these four nets done, just as the other three "skippers" were responsible to get their own picked. Whatever work I didn't finish, the others would have to add to their own.

We picked the fish from two nets, Chad and I, nets both about six hundred feet long. With our legs braced, the skiff yawing and pitching, both of us were barely able to hold the net in place long enough to pull it up and and pick whatever unfortunate fish were caught there. At some point, we began to care nothing about the fish; we only knew that if we removed them all from the nets, we could go back home. We held the bow into the waves, but every wave threatened to swamp us. Still, I did not leave; responsibility held me there. Toward the end of the second net, long past exhaustion—a feeling you don't identify when you're any kind of skipper—another skiff appeared over the crest of a wave and signaled us out of there.

No one called me foolish for hanging on. All of the others were working in the same conditions and they did not quit. But I knew better. Anything could have happened. And any one of those things could have easily determined the length of Chad's life and mine.

This is part of what I know of being a skipper. But my experiences are small-scale. With a larger vessel, the pressures are magnified. You alone hold the lives of two, three, or four people in your hands. Your boat payments and insurance costs run you in the tens of thousands every year—your boat must catch fish. You must manage a potentially volatile mix of personalities and work habits. You must have extensive knowledge of navigation, weather patterns, fishing regulations; you must be able to operate and repair to some degree the array of high-tech electronics that are the brains of the boat; the list goes on.

Why does anyone willingly hoist and carry such a load? There is another side, of course. To state it positively, there is independence in skippering, a degree of autonomy seldom found in other professions. You alone control the life within your ark. You can decide where you are going to fish, when the boat goes, how fast it goes, how long and hard the crew will work, how long everyone sleeps, the weather conditions you will work in, the degree of risk you will take, the kind of food you will all eat . . .

All of these pressures and freedoms are true for both men and women who operate their own vessels. But when women are skippers, the position and the stories deepen and intensify. As they speak, you will hear this. These women speak for themselves, however. They do not represent a movement or a trend; only a handful of women across the state have taken their role in commercial fishing this far. Even then, the fallout rate is high. Of the four who tell their stories here, only two still run their own fishing operations: Mary Jacobs and Leslie Smith. Cinda Gilmer moved with her five children to Florida while her husband continues to fish in Alaskan waters; Debbie Nielsen, who lost her life partner in a tragic sinking, will return to skippering when she is ready.

Mary Jacobs

Mary Jacobs is a legend around Kodiak Island and beyond. Since 1979 she has owned and run her own vessel in salmon, herring, and halibut. Known as "Macho Mary," she consistently finishes most seasons in the top 10 percent of the fleet and says, without apology, "I want to beat everybody out there." Tom, now her former husband, is also a fisherman.

The first year I fished, I could see there was lots of sexual pressure going on. After one year of fishing and being at the whim of a guy, that was enough for me. My idea was to avoid it by running my own boat and giving that opportunity to other women to avoid that situation.

There were very few women fishing when I first started, but the ones who were fishing were friends of mine. When I got my own boat, there were these women that were the orphans in the fishing industry. They started fishing through connections, boyfriends or husbands, but they didn't want to keep those connections anymore, so they were real obvious people to take. And you just couldn't get better people.

We had four very compatible people that liked each other, and I probably should have accentuated that part of it. I didn't realize how important that was. I had only worked with John [former partner] before, and he was somewhat of a yeller, so that had rubbed off on me. I thought that was the way you were supposed to do it. And I remember telling Vicki, "Stop smiling!"—wanting things to be really serious, just keep it to business. They were good-natured about it, but I still get teased about what a tyrant I was that year. And I had no business being a tyrant because I didn't know anything more than they did. Now that's one of my priorities—the interpersonal. It took me the next year to realize how important it was to have four people who could get along, because the boat was really tiny, twenty-nine and a half feet. You could turn around once on the floor space. There were three and a half bunks. Vicki got the half bunk. And she was quite happy with it. She'd either have to have her hair hanging off the end of the bunk going onto the stove or her feet hanging off. She burned a few pairs of socks on the stove while she slept. We had no head, just a bucket out on deck and the rail. We went to tie up with one boat one time and they didn't want us there because we were too dirty. But we were young enough and enthusiastic enough that that part of it didn't bother us.

My first year, 1979, we had a lot of things to learn about, had a lot of breakdowns. The first set the exhaust blew up and we had asbestos everywhere. We had to go in and repair that. And then we went out and caught a bedsprings on Broken Point as our second set. And then the third set we caught another net. We spent six hours on the gill net and ended up with our seine all cut up. And our hydraulics are broken down, we're fixing them. It was bad. We just couldn't physically pull the seine off the gill net, so we just had to wait for the tide change. We were lucky, though; we were just on the fish every week. We didn't catch as many fish as we should have when we were there, but we were in the right place a lot. So we had a really good year, the first season. When you have a little boat like that you're an underdog anyway. Nobody expects that much out of you. We had fun just surprising people when we did catch fish. Nobody really took us seriously when we started out. I think they did by the end of the summer.

Anyway, the following spring I was looking for new crew. I ended up hiring Cinda [Gilmer] and Liza. I was going, "Oh this is so neat having four such different people, people that would never normally be together. It's going to be a really interesting summer." There was Cinda the religious one, Liza was a biker—came to work on a Harley, really tough gal, wasn't afraid to do anything. I figured she could be engineer. Cinda certainly had enough brains and confidence to run the skiff, and Mary Relier was fantastic on deck and a fantastic web person. So I had all the potential of a good crew. But we could not get along. It was a nightmare. There were just all these little things that were bothering us about each other. The boat seemed really small that year. We all had our different interests. I just realized at that point you've got to have a good time, you've got to enjoy being with each other. And that became a priority of mine, rather than just qualifications. And that is something I have kept as a priority to this day.

I was never intimidated by how small our boat was; I was only frustrated that I couldn't carry a big enough seine. But then I probably don't intimidate very easily. It's a challenge. If someone tries to intimidate me, I'm more likely to try to turn it around on them. I just get goaded by it. But I saw many times I didn't catch as much fish as someone else just because I didn't have a big enough seine and the boat was too slow—the same reasons everyone else goes to bigger boats. You just want more efficiency. And there's only so much time you can put your crew through that misery of having only five gallons of water on the boat, with no way to get cleaned up or use a head or anything like that.

So that fall I bought a new boat. Vicki and I were sitting on the flying bridge thinking about what to name it. We were talking about how when we first started it was the Dark Ages and now we were accepted in the fleet. "What's that period after the Dark Ages? The Renaissance!"

So that's how we came up with the name *Renaissance*. I'm on my third *Renaissance* now. It's a fifty-one-foot boat with refrigeration, auxiliary engine, all those things.

I like the dynamics of having the women together. Other crews in other seasons got along much better than that first year. And you don't have problems of ego on the boat like you usually get when one guy's surrounded with women. I knew we could all get along. We just talked about the same things, had similar interests; we could take a sponge bath without worrying who was seeing you. It just seemed to work fine. But I was getting over the point of just always taking women. I was looking for a skiffman one year and Fred Sargeant came down looking for a job. I didn't know who he was and asked him if he had any experience. He just kind of smiled. Course he had been on boats since he was two. He was just really wonderful. He was the first guy I hired. We'd do silly things to him, like wash out our underwear and hang it up on the flying bridge then send him up there to get something. But it was pretty amazing that someone who has lived his whole life in fishing under traditional terms could have no problems with the situation that we had. I guess Fred broke the barriers there, the fact that you could have a guy on the boat and it could be fine.

There's another thing I like about having all women on the boat. I've seen it when we have three women and one man. Then we'll sit back and let a guy fix things. When there are all women on the boat, we figure out how to fix it ourselves. I like being forced to have to do that. Although it's been nice the past couple of years to have Tom [husband] fix things. I mean there is both sides to it. I've gone through that, and maybe proven I can do it, but if there's a good mechanic on the boat, I'm just as glad to let him fix things. Last year I had a good mechanic, and I can just concentrate on the fish-catching part of it. If you have to be fixing things too there's times when you can't see what's going on. And I think with a boat as large as mine with as much complicated mechanics, it's just a good idea to have a good mechanic on the boat and to have the separate roles.

I would say I run the boat differently than men. I think it's more of a democracy. You'd probably have to ask my crew. I try to listen to the crew for their suggestions because they often have good suggestions. But we have a way of voting that goes back about ten years. You have five votes. You vote with your right hand for, your left hand against. You can split your five votes up any way, and so, if I'm deciding about traveling someplace or staying where we are, then I say, "Okay, right hands for traveling, left hands for staying." Or making one last set at night. That's another one we often have votes about. If I feel strongly for doing it I'll vote five for doing it and zero for not doing it. Then we count up all the votes and see how it comes out. Then I do what I want to do anyway.

I don't know if other people see me out there as representing women. Maybe. I guess I'm used as an example, but mostly because I'm just about the only one. I don't feel like I represent anybody but myself. And the only pressure I feel is what I put on myself. I want to do as good as I can. I want to beat everybody out there, doesn't matter—woman or man.

I didn't have any idea of what I was going to be doing twenty-five years ago. And in fact everybody in my family, my cousins, my sister, everybody has gone a pretty standard route, finishing college, getting professional jobs. But it's getting to the point where my family no longer thinks this is a lark or expects me to settle down and finish college some day. It's just so satisfying to be out around the island, seeing the different places. It's a job with a view. We go to these beautiful places. I'm with some really wonderful adult people on a day-to-day basis and we have a really good time. I get away from the phone, the responsibilities of the house. I don't have to cook for myself—I have a cook on the boat. There's some really nice things about the lifestyle. And making money at it. If I could find a replacement that could do all of these things, I'd probably be doing something else, but it gives me a lot of freedom. I think just having my own money, getting away from dealing with children twelve months out of the year are a couple of things that push me back to it.

I can't imagine still fishing ten years from now, though. We talked a little about all of us being out there in wheelchairs! I don't know. I want to fish herring this year and lease the boat out for salmon, and I'd like to keep the boat, to fish herring. I'd like to be able to stay fishing, keep my hands in it, keep making some money at it. But I really don't want to be away from my young kid for five months. So for this year that's what I'm going to try. And hopefully I can do that for two years, and then she may be getting old enough to take her out on the boat after that. Keep involved in it that way. I don't know. I don't know if I'm going to stay with it or not. I've been taking one year at a time for a long time. I don't know how long that's going to last.

Leslie Smith

Before she began setnetting in one of the roughest areas around Kodiak Leslie Smith owned and ran her own seine boat. Though she had only crewed a few seasons on a seine boat, she so hated the humiliation of walking the docks each season that she was willing to take the risks. Her seining career was anything but routine.

The last boat I fished on I kept thinking in my mind the skipper was doing dumb things. I wouldn't have done it that way. I thought we should have gone here when we went there and I thought we should have done this in the set when we did that. I started getting myself into trouble by saying things. Then I realized that if I'm going to be a good deckhand, I've got to keep my mouth shut. If I can't keep my mouth shut, I should just get my own boat. So that's what I ended up doing. Which sort of coincided with turning thirty, I think, and realizing I didn't really have a pot to piss in. I really hadn't done anything in my life. It was sort of a step into the abyss for me, because I'd only been crewing for three years and I didn't have a real vast knowledge of the whole operation. It's not just the fishing, but what did I know about diesel mechanics and hydraulics and electrical systems, all that stuff you really need just to survive, just to keep your boat from sinking or being incapacitated. I didn't know much!

It was that and then really dreading the thought of looking for another job. I didn't think there were too many jobs in Kodiak available to me because I always had this feeling that I wanted to learn more and more. And if I stayed with the same person, I wouldn't be learning more. So I wanted to get more and more experience and see different styles of fishing so I could learn. But I really didn't want to have to look for a job again, to go through beating the docks.

Beating the docks was the worst thing. After I did it for a while I realized that probably there's only 15 percent of the boats that you even have a possibility of being hired on because the rest of them will not hire women. Mostly because their wives won't let them or there's another woman on the boat already or they're just flat out sexist—they don't want women. But between those three factors, the number of boats you could get hired on was so slim that it was discouraging. But first you had to find out which boats those were. That means walking the docks. I'm not a real outgoing person anyway, so it was hard for me to go up to strangers and ask for a job. You walk on a boat and there's a bunch of old fishermen sitting around and you ask for a job and they look at you like—I don't know—they laugh at you, they start to play games with you. It was just very degrading. All the other women friends I have who have fished had to go through the same thing too.

That first year I worked for Mary [Jacobs]. That was really exciting for me. The reason I feel really lucky is that she was still in her all-women phase. We were out there, and here's a woman running a boat with an all-woman crew and we were doing it. We were doing it just as well as anybody else in the fleet, so I never felt intimidated in thinking, "Oh a woman can't do this, can't figure it out, or is not capable of it." So it was a good place to start.

If I had not fished with a woman, I probably would not have gotten to the point of thinking I could run my own boat that quickly, if at all. Fishing with her and seeing that she was doing it made me think, "Hey, if she can do it, I can do it!" It's funny because after I got my own boat, I had several friends, guys who were deckhands who worked on other boats, who then looked at me and said, "If she can do it, I can do it." And then they went out and were ready to make the move. That's kind of how it works. You just have to have that something to push you over the edge.

I ended up buying a boat I had worked on, this little wooden seiner, thirty-six feet, called the *KikiTuk*. That was a real turning point in my life, making that decision to buy a boat, because I didn't know what I was doing. I had to learn everything. I was a bit overwhelmed by all of it. Actually the most difficult thing about the whole summer turned out to be something I had never even anticipated, which was handling the crew. It never even entered my mind as being something that would be the problem. But I went through a lot of crew. When you have a little stinky wooden boat and you're a woman who doesn't exude a lot of self-confidence, first of all you're not getting a lot of people asking you for a job. So my first crew was an illegal foreigner and his friend and then this woman who was just sort of starting out too.

We went over to Uganik Bay. I was late for the opening, of course, because I was trying to get the boat ready to go. We were driving out to Uganik and the boat was leaking really bad. My alternator wasn't working so my bilge pumps weren't working. I didn't know what was wrong except it wasn't working. Alternators are kind of mystery items anyway. So I had one crewman out on deck pumping at all times, manually pumping. I didn't have a clue where to go, really. I decided to go to Packer's Spit. It was an easy place to start. And there was nobody else there. I got there the day it was supposed to close. I made a couple of sets and I was in the third set of my career when the troopers drove up in a Boston Whaler. Only I didn't know it was the troopers. Here come these guys and I'm the only boat in the bay fishing. And they looked at me and they said, "Do you have a license to do this?" "Well, course I do!" Then, "Do you know what time it is?" And I thought, "Oh shit, it's closed already and I'm still fishing." Closing was at nine, and it was seven something. But I got really scared and I said to my crewman, "What time is it?" He looks at his watch and says, "Oh, 7:30." And I go, "Oh, I guess it's 7:30." And the troopers go, "No, it's 7:33." You know, they were just fucking with me. And they came on board the boat, while I was fishing, in the middle of the set. They interrogated my crew, took them aside, busted them all for illegal licenses. They had bought residence licenses when they weren't residents. They really harassed me. Now I would never let it happen like that, but I was so scared at the time I didn't know what was going on. So I had to go back to town so my crewmen could go to court. That was my first day!

I lost those two crew, then I got a couple more, some college guys from back East who I really liked and got along with and had a good time with. But then they decided they could make more money working in the cannery, which made me feel good. So they quit. Then I ended up going to the B & B Bar and picking up someone out of there. He turned out to be this guy who had just gotten out of jail. This guy was my skiffman, and after a week he decided he needed to go to town so bad that he deliberately ran the outboard without oil so it would seize up and we'd have to go to town.

I just bumbled along through the summer and I ended up catching what the fleet average turned out to be for the year. I didn't have time to stop and think about anything. I just kept going.

I think a lot of things happened to me because I was a woman and because I didn't have a reputation. I didn't have confidence. I gained that confidence over that first year, but I still never got good crew because I never got to the point of having a good reputation. And I never had a good boat.

Well, I sold that boat after two years. I had gotten together with my husband, Jeff, by then. My father came up to visit and between the two of them they decided that I shouldn't be driving around in this funky little wooden boat. They coaxed me into looking for a new boat. So we went to Cordova and bought a fiberglass boat, the *Midnight Rider*, a thirty-eight-foot Delta. I rebuilt the engine in that before the season started.

That third year I hired a couple of my women friends for crew. And we actually had fun that year. They were friends of mine, we had a good time. It was hard for me to hire women because I felt like my lack of experience in a lot of the mechanical-type things meant I wanted to hire someone that knew about it. And there weren't many women that knew about it. So usually I would look for a guy that had some mechanical abilities. And that's still kind of a problem. Even setnetting there are a lot of women that want to get into fishing and they always come to me, being a woman, to hire them. But it's like, well that's nice, but I really need a strong guy. I need someone who knows how to fix outboards and has some mechanical skills—so I feel bad because it doesn't always work that way. Most women don't have those qualities.

There were problems being skipper at times, and I think it happens with all skippers. The crew can turn against you. You're on the flying bridge and they're down below talking about you. And if you go down below they go up on the flying bridge. They may not be your friends all the time. It can be lonely.

And then the gender dynamics on the seiner are difficult. There's four people, so there's me and then I could hire three guys, but I would definitely be outnumbered. They get together and go against you. Or you could hire two women and one man, but that would get polarized, the women against the men. Then with three women and one man, a lot of guys aren't going to be able to handle that—"the women are out to get me" kind of thing. So it really comes down to personalities. Okay, here's a good skiffman, but is his ego going to be able to handle being on a boat with three women when the other guys in the fleet start talking about him or whatever. It's really hard to get that all worked out. You have to figure out the personalities. That can be a hard thing on a seiner, especially when there's women and men together. Trying to get a combination that'll last, that'll work.

That first year turned out all right. But I felt a little disappointed because I felt I should be getting better and better each year at some progressive rate, but I still ended up average for the fleet. I held my own. And I was still learning. But by then I'd gotten together with Jeff. I got pregnant and I was thirty-four years old. I thought, "Gee, if I'm going to have a family, I'd better do it now." And that became a priority. Fishing was great for a career. I feel bad that I didn't become more accomplished at seining, but the timing was just wrong. If I had started fishing when I was younger, I would have gotten to that point. But still it was the choice I made to have a family. I made the choice and I'm really happy with it. I love my family, I love my kids, and seining was exciting and a real challenge, but there are so many things about it that are unappealing to me now that I didn't really want to go back to it.

For one thing, it's a really miserable lifestyle. You have to get up at 3:00 A.M. Kodiak has a really long season; we fish from first of June till end of September. Dealing with a crew for that long of a period, living with whoever they are, right in your face, for four months is hard.

The fishery really changed in the few years that I took off to have my kids. It really changed in the whole feel of it. Part of it had to do with the successes of '88 when a lot of people upgraded their gear and equipment, so it became a very high-pressure thing. And everybody turned into an asshole. I've heard the stories and have been out with my husband on a few trips while I was having the kids and pregnant. And I saw it. It used to be much more of a gentleman's type of thing. But the attitudes changed and the management changed. It's really brutal and competitive. It's just incompatible with raising babies. You talk to people in other parts of the state—"Oh, you can bring your kids on the boat. Lots of people do it." They do it in southeast Alaska, in Cook Inlet; that's fine, but I wouldn't want to do it here. I've been out there, and the age my kids are, one and three, it's really incompatible. I don't think they would like it. I wouldn't like it! You can't be competitive and be taking care of these little ones at the same time.

I never was one of these people that was ultracompetitive. When you're seining, you're kind of on the cutting edge. You're out there competing. It's a very male kind of thing to do. You're just out there like an animal; you're trying to outwit everybody, trying to find the fish.

Then, I don't know, when I had babies you get into this whole maternal mode. It's really kind of an opposite thing. I don't really care about being a predator. I'm in a nurturing role right now. They're kind of opposite ways of being. Not that you couldn't do it, I guess, but I've lost interest in that.

Debra Nielsen

Between the ages of seventeen and twenty, Debra hitchhiked up and down the Alaska Highway seven times. In between those trips she traveled alone through much of Asia. She eventually landed in Kodiak and began a fourteen-year career salvaging boats and commercial fishing with her partner, Red Nietupski. Like many women in fishing, she started as cook and deckhand, moved to skiffman in their seining operation, then took the final pioneering step of owning and running her own vessel.

At the end of the first five years of fishing with Red, I started to feel like I wanted to do more than just cook and work deck. I'd watch him train and retrain skiff people. They'd be gone in another season or two. I kept telling him I wanted to run skiff. At that time there weren't any other women running skiff. I guess a couple of other women on the island were just learning at the same time as me. Finally he said, "If you run skiff, I'll never find a guy who'll cook while you're in the skiff." And that was it. After that I said, "Well, I'm going to be in the skiff. He'll have to learn how to cook." That was the turning point in my own achievement individually from him, and that happened when I was about twenty-four. So I began running skiff for the seine operation.

To explain it, it's a separate boat from the fishing vessel. It's a smaller boat—they were around fifteen feet to twenty feet at that time—and it has an outboard. Where we fished on the mainland, it was really difficult because the tides would go out quickly. You had a lot of wind chop on the beach, and if you came in too close to the beach, you could get thrown on the beach. The waves get really rough sometimes. You have to make a lot of judgment calls. You have to have some expertise as far as what the concept of catching the fish is all about. And you have to be able to get yourself out of trouble if you get into trouble with the use of power. Most skippers didn't feel comfortable putting a woman in that position. There is a protective sort of male-female thing that kicks in too. It isn't just about skills. That's something I've run into time and again in the fishery. I think women will get their back up and say, "You won't let me." But when you talk to the men, they say, "Well, I don't want her to get hurt." It's something I've come to understand. The only way to bypass that is to be so skilled that they have no fear. And that's what I got to.

I'm only five feet tall and I weigh one hundred pounds and so men have a protective instinct toward me. I've had to surmount that my whole life to actually get in and do anything. The only way I've been able to get past it is by being quicker and knowing what I'm doing. It's about leverage. You just have to know to get a big pipe; you have to know how to do things. You have to slow down. You have to use your head in a different way and your body in a different way. I think it's important that people know how small I am because if I can do it, it means any woman can do it. Oftentimes we do let that get in the way of what we think we can achieve. But it has to do with the use of power, the laws of nature, the laws of motion. I can move an eight-hundred-pound crab pot across the deck if the sea is with me. And I've done it by myself. You just have to wait for the right sea and guide it. Be fast, don't let it tip this way, let it tip that way. Of course there are times when you're thinking, "This might not work." But 99 percent of the time it works. It's just a matter of using what's around you.

At about the ten-year period of time Red and I were together, I started running the seiner by myself. I had all-men crews. I thought I wouldn't have to worry about things like sexual harassment since I was the skipper, but I did have situations where I was approached sexually by the crew members. They didn't seem to realize they could get fired. They were being basically just natural animals in a situation where they were out at sea with somebody for three months or two months and they liked the person. They were just being real comfortable. One time I had a crewman crawl in my bunk. I'm the only woman around and there is an admiration thing that kicks in where people really do like each other. If you work really closely with someone, after a while you say, "Wow, I really like this person. I like who they are, the way they do things." On two separate occasions I had to say to them, "This isn't going anywhere, but I really do like you. You're fine and we can fish the season together." Afterwards there wasn't any problem. There could have been, depending on the caliber of the person. But these people were just really fine people. It really wasn't a rejection, because I did validate who they were. You have to be sensitive about how you put it. I think that's one of the things some women have a hard time with. I don't have any problem with the attraction that men and women have for each other. I don't have any problem with that on boats. I'm not going to sleep with anybody, but I don't have any problem with the attraction. I think it's healthy and natural and you just work with it.

I've had crews where I had two women, myself and another woman, and two men aboard and everybody got along splendidly. Everybody else in the fleet thought we were all sleeping together because we were having so much fun! We all got on so good, but nobody was sleeping with anybody. We were just working together and liked each other. And it's almost like "No, this can't happen, not for three months on a little boat where you don't even have a toilet." You're working so closely together; your bunks are right there; you have to get up and get dressed and undressed, go to sleep all in the same little space. But we just loved each other.

I had another season where I had an all-female crew in '90 and they were just delights. It was just wonderful working with all women. I had never done that before. I just basically would hire whomever was competent, so I worked with all-men crews, mixed crews, and all-women crews. And it was really a fun season. That year when I had an all-female crew, we actually put in a new engine. We took out the old engine and put in a new engine by ourselves. And that was kind of a big deal. There really aren't any systems in place in this town to help you do that. I was intending to just go find somebody and pay them to do it, but there was nobody you could pay to do it. So we ended up doing it ourselves and learned a lot. I think that was one of those things that made me realize how much I had learned. It was great for the women to accomplish that then go fishing too.

I think the difference when you have an all-women crew versus a mixed crew, there's a little tighter camaraderie. There's just a tighter friendship level you can achieve. Everything's so relaxed. Also, in general, with my little boat, I get a higher quality of woman asking for a job than I do men because the men tend to go to the best boat they can find, the biggest one, the most bells and whistles. The women will often look for a job and not find one on that boat, but then they'll hear that I hire women and they'll come to me. Often they're the cream of the crop. The crew I'm speaking of now, one of the women was a certified welder, one was an avalanche control skier and an EMT, and the other one had just been to mechanic school. So they were just a package you could never have asked for. So I was really pleased with the caliber of women I would run into fishing.

When fishing with all men, it was sometimes a little difficult. I think because of my size and because of just the all-male quality of fishing in a way. But the kind of men who would come and ask me for a job had a quality about them that was a little more expansive to begin with. I really had very few problems over the years with men working with me. If there was a problem, it was often just a personality conflict, which happens between people anyway. Especially when you get four people in a really small environment and then they're asked to achieve very difficult things day after day when they're wet and they're tired and they're cold. They're working twenty hours and then they're pitching fish. It's just a lot of work. In any of those environments you're going to have some conflicts that arise. But we did fairly well.

I remember once we had had a really rough day. A lot of things had broken down and it was really rough and really cold. I had kind of removed myself and was on the bridge and was running somewhere because we had caught no fish that day. I was feeling kind of low. One of the men, in an all-men crew, just walked up and draped his raincoat over my shoulders and put a cup of coffee down on the seat. It was one of the nicest tributes I'd ever received because he just saw real clearly—and that's what usually happens on a boat anyway—people see your effort and a kind of continuity of integrity.

Whether someone likes you or not is sometimes a matter of temperament, but whether they respect you isn't something you can make them do. Male or female you have to be worthy of respect. Some people who have to scream all the time or do things all the time that are demeaning to the crew, they're not going to get that respect. I'm not saying I haven't screamed at different times when there was stress or when trying to get things to happen or just trying to make sure someone could hear me. I have, but I think after the first season or two, I started to learn the less you do that, the better off you are. Toward the end I didn't have much use for it at all. It isn't a tool that people should use continually.

When I first started fishing, I think I was seen as a high seas female pirate because I used to rob creeks [catch fish illegally near the mouth of a stream] with Red. A lot of the boats used to do it then. It was before Fish and Game had a lot of control and it was before there were a lot of environmental issues about it. It was something that was kind of like a "boys will be boys" attitude that people had about it then. It changed during the time we fished together. We used to have a great time doing it. But as we learned and changed, I understood that my own fishing career was going to be taking place in a totally different environment. You just have to be more globally environmental than twenty years ago when I first got up here, when it was completely wild and everybody was doing whatever they wanted.

Now, I think basically my reputation is that you're going to learn something when you go out fishing. You're probably going to have a little bit different quality of fishing than on most boats. That's one of the things that make it nice to go fishing with me: people get to experience more than they would if they went on some other bigger boat to make more money. When you fish on a small boat, you can't expect to make the money you make on a bigger boat. I make sure the crew knows that coming into it. They pretty much have those factors in mind. We get on pretty well because the honesty is there. I don't try to fool them. I think this approach is more effective. I've had such warmth at different times. I remember one year my crew didn't want to come back to town. We got to the town bridge and they were trying to turn the boat around. I was so pleased. We hadn't had that outstanding a season, financially. They were saying, "There's got to be one more fish out there! Just gotta be! We can't go back yet!" And I felt the same way. It was like "We really don't want to go back to town, but I guess we have to."

Somebody said something that was really funny to me. I was pregnant at the time. He was a skipper and an old friend. He said, "Well, what are you going to do with your permit and boat now?" I said, "Well, I don't know. I'm not sure. I probably will just hang onto it." And he said, "Yeah, you should, because what if you have a son. You'll want to pass it down to him." And I thought that was so funny. Here I am a female skipper, a boat and permit owner, and if I have a *son* I'll pass it down to him! I just looked at him and smiled and said, "Or a daughter."

I'm looking forward to teaching my daughter, Danica, full-spectrum knowledge and having her understand power by teaching her how gears work. Having her understand power by letting her know from the beginning she can be confident with movement. And I think that that's something we need to teach our daughters. Because otherwise we're raising children who have these huge gaps which are damaging to them. When they look at a world that is often built by equipment— and it's built by equipment, not sex organs. So they need to learn how to use the equipment. Then they won't be afraid, they won't be limited. I don't see that as a gender issue. I just see it as an area of expertise or knowledge that we're not encouraged or taught. I think just the basic things of knowing how to use a screwdriver or knowing where water comes from. All of those things, it's really important that little girls and little boys know. It's the physical world. And that's something that's become layered in modern society. Oftentimes boys and girls, neither know. And it makes them vulnerable.

All that time I was working, I've always had a joy of learning. It wasn't satisfied by things I could have easily achieved, like book learning. I could just sit down in a clean library and pick up a book and read it. But I really like the feeling of totally integrated learning. You still have to look at a book, but you're actually applying the knowledge. You feel that knowledge and it burns through you. You feel it in your muscles and you feel it in your soul. You really are doing it. It's a total experience, a living experience. And I think that's what's so different about fishing—it's totally integrated. You don't get the soul part until after you get the knowledge. It's the reward. Because you can't even go out there and float on the water and see that sun on the horizon or the moon rise at night unless you know how to turn on that engine and everything's running and you know the injectors are okay and you know that the fuel filters are clear and you know where you're going and how to navigate and your crew knows what they're doing, the whole thing. It's a totally integrated experience.

Cinda Gilmer

After landing a job and a place to stay on the first day she arrived in Alaska, Cinda walked the docks for whatever jobs she could get—learning to mend web, painting boats, running a forklift at a cannery, working the deck on a salmon seiner. The next season she worked as skiffman for Mary Jacobs, then after two seasons tried merging her fishing career with her marriage, with mixed results.

I got married that winter and went to Sand Point [in the Aleutian Islands]. Tyler was a biologist and was working for Fish and Game in False Pass. With our wedding money we bought a skiff and I commercially fished halibut out of our skiff. I had fished halibut before, so I had some experience. It was interesting because out there no women are on the local boats. I don't think any woman wanted to be on the boats. I hired another woman to help me—we were quite a novelty. Men were always trying to help us. They go, "Oh, we can cut the heads off those halibut for you." They were really funny, and really nice, more than helpful.

The only time we had a hassle was with one guy. We were getting some ice. He wanted to pull up to the dock so he could get ice and our skiff was in the way. This little gal, Betty, that worked with me was the wife of a Fish and Game guy too. And she's about 4'11", from Mexico. I wasn't there, I was in the cannery. But I see this guy, and we're right in the way. There's nothing she could do. He's just got to wait. So he started yelling at her and she started yelling at him in Spanish. I don't know what she said or if he could understand it or what, but he just left her alone after that. I don't know if he thought she was going to throw knives at him or what, but she was feisty! We were running out to where we were going to set our lines, cutting our bait, did up all the hooks, set them all—'cause it's all by hand. Then we came back in. Then she told me she had never baited a hook before in her life. She had never cut the fish—nothing! She told me afterwards. She never said boo the whole time, just did it. In fact, she got seasick in that skiff. She'd just throw up over the side and keep on working.

The first time we got back to the dock and we were docking the skiff, the wind was blowing real hard. So I spun the skiff around and she was going to jump out. And she jumped out with the line to the skiff. She got to the dock, but she didn't have her momentum going. So she's falling backwards and she turned around just in time to grab the rail of the skiff. She's 4'11" and she's hanging. This is all I see, her hanging on the rail of the skiff, her big brown eyes. I ran up there to grab her. I just grabbed her by the pants and dumped her into the skiff like that. And all the water that was in her boots ran up through her rain gear. So this is her first day fishing. She came back still the next day. She was tenacious. I had more respect for her.

I had decided to take the summer off, but Tyler encouraged me to halibut fish. He really pushed me to halibut fish. I did not want to halibut fish. At that time I felt like halibut fishing was no-mind work; you're just an extension of the equipment. But he really encouraged it, so I did it. And he said, "Oh you won't catch many halibut" and all this. And after the first day I was ready to kill Tyler, 'cause we got all these fish. Packed our little skiff full of fish! I'm pulling all by hand, all these skates, and catching all these fish. I mean we were catching halibut bigger than Betty was. We didn't have any way to pull them into the skiff—they were so heavy. And alive like that in the skiff, they'd kill you. We didn't have a gun. So I just shoved a stick up through their gills and tied them off to the boat. We got to be famous in Sand Point. We were very successful at it, just what I didn't want to be.

But the next year I went back out there and fished halibut again, mostly just to be there because Tyler was. We felt that was important for our marriage. The second year I did it just the same as the first. We made some money off it, $8,000 or $10,000. That's a lot of halibut to pull by hand. But see neither of our husbands could even touch a line because they were Fish and Game. They could ride out in the skiff with us, but that was it.

Then we started looking for permits for drift gillnetting for salmon. One permit came up that fall. A guy said whoever came up with the money first could have it, a boat and permit. We came up with the money and then he gave it to another guy. These permits were hard to come by then. So we were Outside when we got a call saying a permit had come up. We flew over there that day, January 1, the same day this permit and boat came up. They said, "If you want it, take it now." So we did. We called up my dad to see if he'd be willing to finance us in the interim. We had to sign for it that day or it would have been gone. And that was for $260,000. But the boat was terrible. It was thirty-six feet. It had been sunk four times; it fell off the barge on the way up when it was brand new. This boat had quite a track record. We got it running that spring and ran it out West. Pretty near sunk it—it really wanted to sink! Here we are fifty hours out to Sand Point. We were out an hour and a half and our whole engine room is being pumped full of water. The in-take hose had come off. That was only the beginning with that boat. It was a nightmare. I had another gal working for me. We lived on the boat with all our valuables packed in case we sunk. Flip, a friend who kind of ran with us, said, "If that boat ever threatens to sink, just radio me and you can step off onto my boat."

I'll never forget that trip, for a couple of reasons. It was the first trip I had made by boat out West. And it was flat, glassy calm. And all the dolphins. Once we got all the problems worked out with the boat, it was a very reassuring, calm feeling the rest of the way out, like this is the way it's supposed to be. And the way the whole permit came about. We just knew that that's what God had for us. Especially since there were only two permits that changed hands that winter.

We just dove into the fishery. I had never fished this way before. On the way into Sand Point, before we had actually begun fishing, I had the experience of getting the net off and on the drum *once,* that was it. Flip was a big help. And this boat did have electronics, hydraulics. I had hired this girl who had fished for four years on her family's boat, gotten a crew share, and all that. It turned out she had sat up in the pilot room most of the time. She was only going to be on there until

June. She kind of rose to the occasion, though. We got into picking fish. She worked at it. We had a four-day continuous opening. We never slept a wink, just worked. It's light all the time so you'd fish all day, go in, and deliver [to the cannery]. The weather was good so you never got a break. Turn around and go right back out. She'd sleep while we were running. I thought she could help run the boat, but she couldn't.

I never considered hiring a man to work with me. I never even thought about it. I guess I didn't want to work with another man. Even if I hadn't been married I wouldn't have hired a man. I've worked in a lot of professions where it was just men and I would be the only female. It was that way in the forest service; it was that way in the logging and the finish carpentry. I always really enjoyed working with men. I think I was very fortunate in that I had very good experiences. I find that if you put one female in a group of men, a female who's capable, whom they respect, they kind of clean up their act. But you have to stay in a noncompromising position. I mean not chasing the men, just doing your job, keeping your nose clean. I've had just really good experiences that way.

That third year, I was so excited! Our first set here at False Pass and Tyler was with me. It was a lot of false anticipation, though. I kind of set myself up to be disappointed, 'cause I am kind of a romantic. And I'll never forget this. We're picking our first set of fish and we'd picked like four hundred fish. I said, "Oh, how about a kiss every four hundred fish?" And he said, "How about if I throw up in your face?" Because he was seasick. And when you're drift gillnetting like that, and you're pulling the fish, then you're just rolling. It can really make you sick. So he was sick a lot that first week.

We had a good first False Pass season, then went north to Port Mohler, and our fishery was changing. Previous to that they just kind of fished around Bear River. That year before only a handful of boats had gone north and had nailed the fish. Flip and I were two of them. But by this second year everyone was getting the idea that these fish were all up there and started running up there. We had horrible, horrible weather. Stormy, snowing, blowing. So for Tyler, who already was feeling sick, it just intensified that. And now we were running a hundred miles to get up there. You'd run up there, fish, and the weather would be so bad you couldn't deliver, so you'd run all the way back.

And you run up and back, so it's very, very grueling. It's the height of the season when the biggest number of fish are caught. It was really wearing on Tyler. And it was just the two of us, but that was normal for this fishery.

I'm one that if anybody goes out, I go out. Nobody really goes out by themselves out there. Mostly you run with a partner. But if one boat would go, I would go. That was hard on Tyler. He'd say, "Oh you always have to be at the front of the line." I never felt that way. I just felt like I had to be where the fish were. Back then I don't think Tyler saw the necessity of that. And the weather was bad that year. You're sitting on that north peninsula so everything just comes straight in at you and you get caught there 'cause you can't get around the corner to the cannery. And you can't ever get any protection. So you're just sitting there getting beat to death sometimes. You just ride it out. So it's hard when it just never lets up. You can be stuck there for days. That invigorates me, though. I get energized by the challenge of it all. It's not hard for me to stay up for anything.

We started sharing a lot of responsibilities with the idea of turning the skipper position over to him. That was the idea. We'd drift and fish all night and we'd take turns doing that. We had a lot of stress just because of different personalities. He would sit up and was supposed to be watching and he would fall asleep. So then I couldn't sleep during my sleep time 'cause he wasn't watching. So that caused a lot of stress. I don't think he trusted me either.

One night we were blowing onto the beach. It was dark out, pitch dark, but we were drifting and catching fish. Then we were getting blown onto the beach, so we had to let go of our net. You have to keep track of the net in the dark, then go and get to the other end of it, tow it around, or do whatever you have to do so you can take up your net and get off the beach. I woke him up. He was just sitting there saying, "Oh no!" I just told him, "Tyler, if you don't want to help, get off this boat." I was so angry because it wasn't a matter of negotiation or somebody being right. But it's awful hard for men to listen to you. He got with it, he helped. We talked about it after, but it was a lot of frustration, a lot of friction.

Later in that summer, we had the only physical fight we ever had. It's very tiring, very grueling by that point, day in, day out. The end of the season is very tough on everyone. It's much darker at night, a lot more wind. The weather goes from bad to worse. You never get off that boat. You never see anyone. Very confining. And we were down an engine, so we were fighting mechanical problems. We could only turn one direction in the wind. I don't remember what he did or what he said, but it was over mending a net out on deck. I always mended the net. I didn't have a crewman to do it, and he didn't know how to do it. I was anxious to teach him, to let him do it. He came out there and he grabbed me by the shirt! I was just like a wildcat. I think I would have scratched his eyes out. I don't even remember what it was over, but that's how tense it was. And once he grabbed me he was afraid to let go. I don't think he knew what I was going to do. I sat out there for a long time. He went in and sat for a long time. Shortly after that we decided to go back. And then I think he was more frustrated at the end of that season than I was. When we got back and I called my dad, the first question he asked was, "Are you still together?" If Tyler had answered he would have said "barely." But I didn't feel that bad about it.

I think it's just frustrating for a man to be in that position where they have to subject themselves to a woman. You're not a person, you're a woman. If I had been a man doing those things it wouldn't have been bothersome. I think it's just natural for men to feel like no matter what, they know more than you do. I think it's hard for men, no matter how experienced a woman is, no matter how much she knows. I always say women think they know everything, but men know they know everything.

I really enjoyed fishing the years I fished. It was really exciting. Part of the excitement was the challenge it was to me. I think now if I fished, like for Tyler, or for anyone else, it would just be a job. But I have to honestly look at myself and say, "Do I want to run my own boat at this point in my life?" Maybe it was a big challenge then. It isn't a big challenge now. It's not that thrilling anymore. But I've been thinking a lot—What am I going to do? I ask myself, What do I really like to do? I love to be on the water. I like the wind blowing in my face. I don't care if it's terrible weather. That doesn't bother me at all. I just like running boats.

5 *"I've Seen People Die"*

This is the fifth day of a blow, a northeast at twenty-five to thirty-five steady, gusting to fifty at least. Fishing in this has been nothing but dangerous and exhausting. We take wave after wave over our bow and stern; we are continually showered by floods of spray, getting soaked through the neck of our rain gear down to the skin. The three of us, Ron, Duncan, and I, are sometimes just barely able to stand and hold the line. Because these waves are steep and close, it's hard to get their rhythm down to keep our balance. We watch every one of them, knowing that any single one could swamp and dump us in this mess of an ocean. I wonder continually if these little life jackets we wear would really float us. We have so much gear on and our hip boots would fill with water immediately, weighting us like an anchor. Could we really stay afloat? In spite of these conditions, we have continued to pick all the nets. It takes so much longer. We've been fishing for thirteen days now. Working in this weather makes each minute seem an agonizing hour. And yet no one even considers quitting.

I don't remember the first time I was scared on the water. Nor do I remember the first time I knew I was in
danger. It's been too long to keep that one memory separate from all the
others. But the elements are always the same: out in an eighteen-foot skiff,
in seas that shrink those modest dimensions yet further, with waves breaking over the stern perhaps, and the skiff heavy with fish. Add to that a motor
that breaks down or perhaps add fog and reefs that disappear. If it is August and the late summer sun has dimmed, add the dark and nets still to
pick and miles to drive with little visibility. Yet somehow it all seems man-
ageable. After all, I am part of what is known as the "mosquito fleet," setnetters who hum and buzz around in skiffs close to shore during the mild-
er summers, not the oceanic crabbers on the multimillion-dollar boats with
names like Pacific Challenger, The Provider, The Dominant, U.S. Dom-
inator, vessels that venture out in the dead of winter to the Bering Sea and
to the westward tip of the Aleutians—the corner of the earth where the
winds congregate only to think up more storms. There, danger is immi-
nent. To tell exactly how close the risks loom, and to tell the whole story,
I must begin with the statistics. My voice may submerge beneath the weight
of the numbers in this chapter. So be it. Without them, we have no scale to
measure the lives and stories that follow.

In 1992, forty-four vessels in Alaska sunk, eighty-seven people were
rescued from sinking vessels, thirty-five died. It was an average year. In
Spring 1988 forty-four died after ice fog moved in and consumed boats and
crew. To put those numbers in perspective, the National Institute of Occupational Safety and Health reports that the annual death rate for all U.S.
occupations is 7 per 100,000 workers. For commercial fishing in Alaska,
the rate jumps to 200 per 100,000, making it the most deadly job in the
country. For crab fishermen, whose season runs through the winter, the rate
climbs to 660 per 100,000, or almost 100 times the national average.

Many fishermen don't know these numbers. I didn't know them myself
until I began to do some research. But no one who fishes in Alaska needs a
set of impersonal statistics, graphs, and computations to remind them of
who they have lost over the years: friends, brothers, cousins, sisters . . .
For many, risk wears a face. That face is often hidden though, hidden beneath a survival strategy that calls mostly upon the brain. To survive, to
fish again and again requires an impassionate calculating, quantifying, and
weighing of risk against reward. The risks, often so calmly enumerated,

are these. Begin with the ocean itself, an unconquerable and unpredictable force. Next, layer on an Alaskan winter, whose winds freeze the ocean spray to instant ice that layers so thick and fast, a single wire can be nearly a half foot in diameter in a matter of hours. Too much ice and the vessel becomes top-heavy and simply, without warning, rolls over and sinks. For the big boats, the solution is baseball bats and crowbars in the hands of crew members, who smash and chip furiously, knowing their very balance in the ocean is at stake.

Other dangers that figure in: deckwork paced with a fury and a recklessness that is almost indescribable. Holly Berry says, "It's like driving down the road ninety miles an hour and you have a split second to make a decision." Gear is flying—hooks can snag you, anchor lines can drag you overboard. Crab pots weighing 750 pounds are muscled around the deck or moved by cranes whose lines sometimes let go. You can be trapped in a pot as it goes overboard. Anything can happen. Even fishing in a skiff, I used to have nightmares about getting caught in the net as it played out over the stern, hissing, at twenty miles per hour.

Reigning over this whole organized mess is the skipper, the demigod who decides the fate of the crew. There is no democracy here. The skipper may be cautious and humane or a modern-day Ahab, possessed and fanatic for the payload, running gear around the clock, depriving the crew of sleep for days on end. Exhaustion and greed drive up the statistics.

Whose idea is this anyway? Who invented this machine? Much of the fuel propelling what seems like fanaticism is the law itself. Fishing regulations carefully establish and monitor the seasons for each species of fish to prevent overfishing. If there is one word to describe each season, it may well be this—shorter. Halibut used to be harvested eight months a year. Then it was reduced to a few twenty-four-hour openings. Because boat payments had to be made, anything short of a hurricane was good enough to fish in. The pollock season has been reduced from two- and three-month seasons to two- and three-week openings. The result? Higher fatalities and the kind of inhuman and seemingly impossible marathons—routinely working twenty-four-hour stretches without sleep—that women like Theresa Peterson have mastered.

This dynamic has recently changed for some of the fisheries, however. A new system of fisheries management based on an individual quota system has replaced the short, intense, and high-risk seasons with longer, less *competitive seasons. Fishermen can pick and chose their weather. The death statistics seem to be dropping.*

Nearly every woman who fishes knows something about the statistics and has stories of her own to tell of fear, danger, exhaustion, death, and injury. Many have seen boats sink. Almost all have seen people injured; some have seen them die; some have been injured themselves. All knew the risks firsthand. Yet somehow each of the more than twenty women I interviewed retained a sense of control over her life on the water. You can hear it in the voices of the four women in this chapter. Despite what seems to be extreme vulnerability—prey to the forces of wind and ocean, isolated, under the absolute authority of the skipper, completely without privacy— you will not hear either the words or the sense of "vulnerable," "victim," "helpless." The weighing and balancing of risk and reward has already been done, and for these women, the rewards have won. High on their lists were money, excitement, and adventure. Even Holly Berry, who barely survived a fall between two boats, would go back in a heartbeat if her permanent disabilities from that fall allowed her to.

This chapter, then, is the story beyond the statistics. It is not just who was hurt and who was killed and which boat almost sunk and why. It is how the survivors, specifically the four women here who stubbornly kept and keep on fishing, live and think and work in the face of risk factors far beyond most people's comprehension.

Theresa Peterson

Despite the inhumane conditions she endures while fishing, Theresa continues long-lining for black cod and remains one of the fastest baiters in the fleet.

I really felt in danger the most when offshore long-lining and these storms would come up. You've got a choice—you either leave your gear in the water or try to get it in. On the first black cod trip I made the weather was so bad it ended up taking us twenty-seven days to get in seventy thousand pounds when normally it would only take ten to twelve days. This is in October and November and into December. We thought we might be celebrating Christmas out there. See, you don't come in till you've got a load. If you come in with half a load, you're not into your profit margin yet and you're not really making much money. You need to get that full load before you come in. So we fished some really horrendous weather.

The first time I saw the rough weather it just kept getting worse and worse. Pretty soon we were in twenty- to twenty-five-foot swells. It was gusting between seventy and eighty miles per hour, so we were in the hurricane winds—it was just screaming. If we left our gear out there, we'd probably lose it all. So the skipper said, "This is going to be hard, but we've got to bring this gear in." We waited till daylight and then we saw these huge waves. The way the boat is built, we were running into it, so it's crashing up over the wheelhouse and then raining down on us. First we brought this longline in. There weren't any fish on it, but I found myself just shaking with fear. You'd have to wrap both your legs around this little stool you were sitting on trying to hold on. It reminded me of the Weebles: "You weeble, you wobble, but you don't fall down!" At that point, trying to bait and run, the gear drops off. You just try to get your gear in and watch out for each other. The waves are crashing on you; the whole deck is awash. The person over at the rail getting the fish on board is getting waves completely over his head. You're watching all this white water and you're not tied on at all. You just have to really watch that there's something to hold onto when the wave comes.

It took about ten hours to get that gear in. That's when I found I had to find my own courage. There's no way back out of that situation and no one can help you at all. And I still had my job to do. I just had to keep doing what I had to do. There aren't any options. You're in that situation and you just kind of get through it and have faith in the boat. Since the skipper felt it was a wise thing to do to get the gear in rather than lose sixty skates of gear, I just kind of had to have faith in the whole operation. One thing the cook told me that really helped me out, something I'll never forget. He looked at me and he could see I was really afraid. He said, "Just think, Theresa, you'll be able to tell your grandchildren about this."

We ended up going into Sand Point after that and staying for seven days. It blew fifty and sixty and seventy for seven days straight. Unbelievable! On the way in from that trip, we were coming in from off Cape

Douglas and it was really nasty again, weather you couldn't fish in—twenty-five- and thirty-foot seas with big rolling white water. We were just trying to make our way to Homer when a rogue wave, from an entirely different direction, came and hit the boat so hard on the side that the whole boat rolled over. The skipper's window up in his wheelhouse actually took in some water. I had been lying down in the foc'sle. The two guys on the upward side came out of their bunks and they and all their gear came out and crashed down on me. Just for a second the boat hovered on its side like that, then came back up. The skipper said that at that point he didn't know if the boat was going to come up or not. Well right away we had to put on our gear and go out to see the damage done to the deck, which was quite a lot. The whole bait shed had been bashed in from the power of the wave hitting it. Our buoy line had all been knocked over and was running out of the scuppers, so right away we had to grab knives and start cutting that. If we didn't, it was only a matter of time before that got in the wheel and we'd be dead in the water. So we were just frantically cutting, massacring our gear. Then there were six tubs rolling around with all the hooks and things. It took a couple of hours out there to straighten it all out. We had to change course again, heading away from Homer because we had to head right into the seas instead of trying to quarter them on our stern. So we kind of just jogged into it that night. We got in that next day and felt like bunch of wounded cowboys stumbling in.

I wasn't really discouraged about fishing after that. It was such a challenge to me and this was by far the best job I had ever had. This was a really highline boat out of Homer. I felt real fortunate to have that opportunity, so it was a challenge that I had to meet. I really wanted to excel in this fishery, so I was determined at that point to not be discouraged by the weather.

I have fished with a skipper that I would call dangerous. He yelled a lot. I had never been with someone that yelled, and I found that really stressful. Just a lot of "Come in! Get it in there!" and cussing and shouting. You're already trying to do the best job you can do and to have the yelling on top of it really set me ill at ease. He did things like cross the entire Gulf of Alaska with the boat not tanked down [the hold filled with water for stability] so we could go a little faster. Boats are made to have some type of ballast, so that disturbed me that we would do that. He said we could go faster. Well, I don't really care about going faster; I want to be as safe as possible.

I had fished last year with him and now this year, and I had known him for years. He does have quite a temper and he used to drink, but he's quit drinking. When he gets out there, though, he gets overwhelmed by the stress. This year, as we came into dock to deliver our fish, we had been up thirty hours straight by then. We laid down for an hour then got up to tie up the boat. We found the hatch on the back tank had been sealed completely when it should have been left open a crack—it was whistling. This air was trying to escape. I was kind of inside and I heard him yelling, "Where's that whistling coming from? What's going on!" Then he saw the engineer standing by the hatch that could explode at any minute, so he just started screaming, "Get away from that!" This was just as I stepped out on the deck. I saw the other two guys running so I turned and ran. I didn't know what was going on, but I knew if they're running, I'm going to run!

At that point he just went flying off on another rampage about "How could you be so stupid! You should know what's going on!" He was just yelling, yelling, yelling. We were tying up the boat, and I was up on the bow. There were two guys on midship and one guy on the stern. Well one of the guys got caught in between the boat and the piling as he was reaching out. I was on the bow and I heard this "crunch," which was him, and I heard him scream. And then he managed to jump back on deck and run to his bunk. He couldn't get up again after that. He ended up getting four ribs broken, injuring his sternum, puncturing his lung. Right away we had to call the paramedics. During this whole time the skipper was yelling, still yelling at the top of his lungs about the whistling and that now Bruce was hurt. I ran up to him and said, "Get a grip! This is not the time!" He looked at me. I think if I had been a guy he would have hit me. He was just unglued, out of control. Here's Bruce, who I've known for twelve years and he's married to my best girlfriend, so I was just really upset, trying to hold back my tears. He's lying there very hurt. Then the skipper came in and started raving at Bruce, "Can't you see what I'm up against? What were you doing out there!"

I think his yelling is part of what caused that accident. Everyone was just a little frazzled. We'd been working hard. We had just laid down for an hour and he's off an another tirade. And so the combination of circumstances make me feel he's a dangerous skipper. He's so driven to catch the most fish, run the most gear. He's a great skipper in terms of catching fish—he had just brought in the most halibut. I really like him in a lot of ways; sometimes he's just as nice as can be, but he just doesn't have a grip on his anger.

One of the main reasons I went fishing this year is because we were behind in a boat payment for our seine boat. We salmon seine in the summers. With the price of salmon being so low, we haven't been able to make it. So my going out has enabled us to make that boat payment. We have children now and we thought we could make it fishing salmon and my husband fishes crab and black cod himself. As it turned out, we need two of us fishing to make it. I was just glad to have the opportunity and the means to go. When you're working and doing well you're making several thousand dollars a day, so that's a great motivating factor. There is a great sense of fulfillment knowing how much we could use this money. When I fished in the eighties and didn't have any children, a home, mortgages, boat payments, making money wasn't as important to me as it is now.

When I go out, I don't really fear for my life so much as fearing getting hurt. Every trip out somebody gets hurt. I don't want to have to go through that pain and misery. This trip out my girlfriend was on the roller bringing the gear in and I was running the boat. The water was rougher than I was comfortable with. I kind of got pushed into it by one of the other guys who was tired of hauling. It was in the middle of the night, about fifteen-foot rollers. I was up there and really having a hard time steering the boat into the waves in the pitch black and my girlfriend was hauling. A snarl came through and it jumped out of the roller and a hook went through her finger pretty badly. I felt somewhat responsible, although it's just one of those things that happens, part of the job. The hook ripped out that time, but sometimes what you have to do if the barb is in your finger is cut the other end and then push it through or grab pliers and pull it through. Usually one other person will stop working and go in to help you get yourself bandaged back up, but then you have to come right back out and work through it with this extra pain.

I think in fishing you can alleviate the risks. There are a lot of derelict boats out there. You can look out in our harbor and see boats not ready for the Bering Sea. A lot of times it's financial pressures—they can't afford to get the proper equipment until they make some money. Then they'll get out in weather that's more than the boat can handle. To me you have to make a series of good choices. Look at the boat, look at its past record, look at who's running it. The skipper has a lot to do with it. See how he feels about safety and keeping the risk factors down and keeping the boat up in good operating condition. You have to follow your own feeling and intuition. If you don't have a good feeling about a boat, don't go on the boat.

One of my favorite quotes has been "The only thing to fear is fear itself." I love the challenge of going out there. It's such a network, a camaraderie of people working together to make something happen. When you get right down to it, driving down the road is actually more dangerous in terms of statistics than commercial fishing. There are so many benefits that outweigh the danger. It's an experience that I'll carry with me through my entire life—heading out to sea, deciding that that's what you're going to do. Once you've made that decision, you have to stand behind it and put the danger factors behind you. There are too many things in life to be afraid of.

Christine Holmes

Despite her experience with the "John Wayne" skipper, Christine continued to fish commercially. After ten years of experience, she knew the risks and worked aggressively to alleviate the dangers through knowledge and training. She took the same approach toward her breast cancer and worked intensively to beat the numbers, even continuing to fish between chemotherapy treatments. After a two-year battle, however, Christine died in May 1996. In the midst of sobering statistics for commercial fishing and for cancer, she continued to face both with energy and enthusiasm.

I noticed in dragging, the two fellows I worked out on deck with definitely watch out for me, not because I'm a woman, but because I'm new and they want me to be the best because I'm working on a good boat. They're pretty into that. Jerry's yelled at me before—"Get the hell out of the way now!" And because it's a new boat to me, you have to learn where to stand. If one of those cables snapped and you're in the bight, it's not going to be pretty. They would much rather I was the way I am than be missing a hand or something. But they've all been through the same thing too. I've fished for a long time, but dragging on such a big boat, there's a lot to it. And a mistake can cost someone else's life.

I've been fishing long enough now—I look at some boats and I don't even bother to apply. If I look at a boat and see the wires looking bad, that the boat's really lacking for paint, or it's really rusty, I'm not going to go out on the Bering Sea on a boat people aren't taking care of. I've had job offers to go on other boats, but it was my choice not to, because it's really easy not to come back from a fishing trip. I just can't see that because I'm a woman I should settle for second best.

When I was Dungeness crabbing, 1986, we had a guy get his finger cut halfway off. I figured since the other two guys on the boat with me had been to Vietnam and seen all these horrible atrocities and whatnot, they could deal with this. But I went to them and said, "His finger's almost cut off!" and they said, "Oh my god!" and they both turned white as ghosts. This was a really old boat, a 1914 double-ender, and there was no medical kit on board. The boat was really poorly equipped. So I ended up down in the galley with this guy. One of the other crew had bought a new thing of tube socks, so I got his finger wrapped up with them and I sat with him for eight hours while we went in to town, keeping him laughing, talking, so he wouldn't go into shock. The Coast Guard couldn't come get him. They were already on another call for cardiac arrest. I was fine when it was happening, but as soon as it was over, I started to pass out. It was awful. Since then I really believe in the North Pacific Vessel Owner's Association; they offer some really good courses, one of which is Medical Emergencies at Sea. I think anytime you can take any kind of marine tech class you're doing yourself a favor.

I've also been rescued by the Coast Guard in my survival suit out here. I had just completed a course here in town on survival and how to disembark a vessel when it's sinking, and it really helped me a lot. I was fishing with a man whose name and boat I won't mention. We were fishing for salmon on the Copper River Flats, which is a very danger-ous area to fish. When the tide is running, there are several different bars. Egg Island is the easiest one. We were fishing way out, probably about five or six miles offshore. I told this guy we should get up early that next morning because I just had this feeling the weather was go-ing to change. My friend Kathy was out fishing the same area. She ran in early. That's one thing I've noticed. Women have intuition. I said to him, "Make sure you wake me up about 5:00 A.M." I woke up like quarter to seven, and he's in the bunk still sleeping. I was, "Come on, we got to go, pick up this net. I don't want to get caught with the net in the water and get a $5,000 fine," 'cause they'll fine the deckhand too. And I just had this feeling: the wind's starting to blow; there's not another boat in sight; everybody's already run in. Well, we got the net on. I think we had about four fish in the net. Thank god we didn't have a full net. We started running for Egg Island. By then the tide was going out and the weather was getting worse and worse. It was just break-ing, big old waves. And the boat was making all these weird noises. I said, "I think we have water in the fuel." So we changed filters and there was a lot of water in the fuel.

Then we started across this bar. The boat is a twenty-eight-foot bow-picker. There's a small window in the cabin. We took a twenty-footer on the stern and the whole window convexed. You know in the *Ter-minator* where the guy takes on the form? The whole window went like that. I said, "That's it! This is fucking crazy! Turn the boat around!" I thought, "If we lose the engines now, that's going to be it." We were able to turn. Well then we had to go out across this stuff, and the boat's going N-N-N-N-N-N. You back it down as the boat gets to the top of a wave. Well, we managed to get out of the breaker patch [concen-trated series of large waves] and there was another little boat out there. It was John, a native I knew. He yelled, "You gotta be crazy trying to cross that thing!" And I'm going, "Yeah, no shit!" And by then we lost both engines. The boat is totally dead in the water. Well Johnny had about enough fuel so he could get in, so he starts towing us. He says, "I'll tow you to Strawberry Island." Well, if Egg Island's bad, Strawber-ry's even worse. So we get to Strawberry and the waves are just huge. And Johnny's boat is only twenty-four feet. This is just crazy! So we called the Coast Guard. They told him they didn't want him to cross the bar at all because we were dead in the water and we were starting to take on water. We had the big aluminum door with the dogs on it closed, and water's just coming in. The Coast Guard said, "I'd like you to prepare to disembark the vessel." And they were sending out the helicopter. I didn't really feel like we were going to sink. But the Coast Guard had answered a call about three years ago where they made a rescue at night and turned out the guy didn't need to be rescued. And when they came down, the rotor caught his antennae and they lost the whole helicopter, crew and everything. So they are really touchy about doing night rescues.

They said, "We'd just as soon come get you guys." So this guy I'm fishing with decides to cut loose from the other boat, which I told him, "Don't cut loose from the other boat because of the way the swell's running." He just cuts the line, right? He didn't even tell the guy who was nice enough to tow us. Well the wave picks us up and drops us down onto the other guy's boat. We drive our bow right through the guy's window. He's still fine, but anyway, we've got to put on our survival suits. My skipper had never put his suit on. I had just finished a class the month before and I always checked my survival suit. He was trying to stand up on the boat and put his suit on. By then I was pretty short-tempered. I said, "Throw it out of the bag like this." And what I do is kick my boots off and throw them in the suit with me. So anyway, he got into the survival suit.

They came to pick us up and they tried to send a basket down, and he goes to reach for the basket. I had to push him out of the way because what happens, and I never knew this until I took a survival class, is that because the rotors create static electricity, if the basket doesn't ground first, before you get rescued, you get knocked out by the electrical shock. So you want it to ground out. Well, because the boat was so small and the seas so big they couldn't set the basket down comfortably. So the guy looks at me from the helicopter and he goes like this, cuts across his throat—no way—and then he looks at me, he holds his nose and starts making this paddling motion. And I was fine till then. To me, fishermen don't belong in the water, we belong on boats. So the only good thing this skipper did, I was looking over the side, thinking about jumping in the water. I was kind of backwards like this, and he pushed me. That was okay. It was strange. You're buoyant, but you go underwater. I wear contacts, and I don't know why I did this but I opened my eyes and I could see the bottom of the boat as the wave came down. And I thought, "What's wrong in this picture?"—well, I'm in it! I'm looking through the water at the boat! I came up and started to do a little backstroke and they sent a diver in. They are so good at what they do. I was probably in the water about five minutes and all of a sudden this diver was there, grabbed ahold of the basket. This wave came down like this and I was in the basket. Kind of like a dead fish in a brailer, like a big king salmon or something.

One thing I have is a tremendous fear of heights. There was a gal working in the helicopter, a technician. She was great. They pulled the basket into the helicopter. She looked at me and she just like dumps me out—"Thanks!" Gosh, they did just a great job. And then they brought my skipper up and he was fine. He had inflated his neck floatation, which I told him not to do when we jumped in the water. You never want to do that until you're in the water because when you jump in you can get whiplash. So he was kind of in bad shape for a couple of weeks.

When we got to the airport here I took off my survival suit. The Coast Guard guy just cracked up because I had made meatloaf the night before. I had half a meatloaf, I had a couple of books, I had a change of clothes, I had two packs of Chips Ahoy cookies, a flashlight, I had everything in my survival suit. The guy said, "How many times have you been rescued?" I said, "This is my first time, but I wanted to be prepared." It was hilarious, but thank god it all worked out. The one interesting thing was we ended up getting the boat two days later. They found it drifting. So it didn't sink.

People think I'm nuts, but I like fishing in the Bering Sea in the winter. It's definitely working on the edge. I like that part of it. But I notice as I get older I take fewer chances. I think maybe in a couple of years it won't be so exciting for me. I don't even know what I'll do next. I've thought, well, I'd like to have kids someday. I don't think I could feel comfortable leaving my kids to somebody else. So maybe I'll try to get my one-hundred-ton license this year and think about working on tugs for four or five years. Those guys make good money. They're just right around in the harbor. They know when they're going to work. They usually work eight-, ten-hour shifts. They know ahead of time when they're going to work, so you could hire a baby-sitter. And you're not going to sink!

I have a lot of buddies that, it's so tough on them to be out there. So many of them have young kids. I'll tell you, as soon as the boat is in town the guys are on the phone to their wives for hours. It's hard for men. I don't know if women realize how tough it is for them to miss seeing their kids grow up. I can see where it would start getting old for me. Right now it's great. I'm really pushing myself. I want to do a good job 'cause I'd really like other gals to be able to do this someday. But I still sometimes wonder, What am I doing here? How long can I go?

I was thinking the other day—I was learning to fly with a guy in his sixties who crashed his plane and died. He was flying supplies to Joe Redington. He taught me a real love of life. Marshall was one of those guys whose answering machine said, "I'm not home. I'm out fishing, flying, and having a helluva good time." Just like he liked to fly, I think some people are meant to be out in thirty-foot seas. They like to feel the wind in their faces and like to see nature at its best and worst. I'm a very spiritual person. I wouldn't say I'm a religious person. I more worship nature. Somehow when I'm out there I feel like it's the closest you can ever get. It's like being in the stomach of Mother Earth, and she had something bad for breakfast. I have times when I've been scared, but I like that feeling. I'm on a boat I feel real confident in. But then again, my friend on another boat just sank. And that boat I have seen come in during some real rough weather. Boy, it was real surprising when it sank—no trace—on a day that wasn't even that rough, up there in Nunivak Pass. I think about those things, but sometimes I just . . . out here fishing on the flats, you'll be out here on the smaller boats; the wind is blowing; you see those fish hit the net. You feel so alive doing that! And I think of people who all their lives never feel that, never really know what it's like to feel that alive. It's a wonderful feeling.

Holly Berry

Holly Berry lives in Kodiak and runs her own gear business—building and repairing crab pots. She knows about the dangers of fishing firsthand.

I worked in fishing about sixteen years, off and on, and I'd still go right now. I like anything that's scary, especially on the water. I've been out in some pretty bad seas and seen some pretty bad stuff.

I remember one time on the *Denali,* the four-hundred-foot processor I was foreman on, we were in forty-foot seas. When you looked up you couldn't even see the sky. I was on wheelwatch. And we got into a tunnel of water. It's odd to get into a tunnel in a ship that size. When that happens, the wave goes completely over the ship. The windows aren't even wet, and you're inside this tunnel. The skipper said to get the survival suits. At that point I thought I was going to die. My heart was going ninety miles an hour, but still it didn't seem to upset me for some reason. Well, we broke through it, which was amazing. The minute we did, the ship started rolling, bouncing back and forth really bad. This all went on in twenty seconds. He looked over at me and smiled and said, "We made it. God was sitting on our shoulder." That's what you call the sea swallowing you up.

I've lost so many friends out there. I've lost fifteen friends on the water. If there's a crab pot, for example, coming on deck and they lose it, he lets go, and you're in heavy seas and the pot's swinging back and forth, they wait to get it in a rhythm so they can stack it. Sometimes they'll lose it and it'll start flapping all over. Then you've got seven hundred pounds coming at you. Well I've seen men jump, I've seen men ride the pot. I rode the pot when it happened to me. When you see it coming at you, all you've got is the railing behind you, so it's either jump or die. Jump onto the pot! Hang onto it! Get out of its way and grab it when it hits the railing, grab on the side of it and go back with it. Then the guys will slow you down. Sooner or later they're going to get ahold of it. But it's better than dying.

I've seen people die. I saw a kid jump right over and we lost him, never saw him again. I saw another kid get crushed on a boat. He was from Kentucky. He came up here to make enough money to go get married, and he was a young boy, about eighteen years old, and he got crushed. I saw it happen. They lost control of the pot and the kid froze. He was green, he got scared, and he didn't know what to do. And the pot hit the railing and then bounced off and hit him, then hit the railing again, so he was real lucky he wasn't three inches over or he'd have been totally squished. He got the rebound, not the initial impact. But he got hurt bad. His spleen got crushed. He was very frail, very small, and I couldn't give him anything. I couldn't give him any aspirin or anything because I had to take his temperature every five minutes. I was on the radio with the Coast Guard with one hand, my other hand was on his chest. It was bad. It was real bad. But he lived, he made it. He made it to Kodiak Hospital. It's amazing. His parents came here and got him, in fact. Took him back. I went up and saw him in the hospital. He was sore and he was upset about this girl. He wanted to marry this girl and bring back a million dollars. His dream had burst.

When I was in Dutch [Harbor], most of my friends I lost were from boats icing up and turning over. You know airports watch wings; well, we watch the boat. I've been iced up bad, been out with my baseball bat chipping ice, but I've never gone over. The crew just constantly on a consistent basis chips ice. You must get up in front, right in front where the wind's hitting you, and you hang on and hit with the other hand and you chip ice off the boat so you don't turn, so you don't go over. And everyone has his own baseball bat. In my day they all had their own names for the bats and everything. I don't know what they do now, they might be using grinders or something nowadays, who knows, but when I was doing it it was bats. I notice when someone comes in my house, I have mine on the front porch. They'll see my bat and they'll laugh and they'll go, "You've been out in St. Matthews?" and I'll say, "Yeah," and they'll look at me real funny, you know.

Yeah, I'm a weird one. Most girls weren't like me. People say, "Aren't you scared? Don't you get nightmares from your accident?" The answer is no I don't. I remember it like it was yesterday. I was on a processor ship and we were tied up down at Old Harbor. There were smaller vessels tied up to us while they off-loaded their crab to us. I was trying to cross from my boat to the *Constance*. It was usually easy for me to cross to another boat to relay messages or fish tickets or just to say hello to someone. I could climb boats like a monkey, but this one night I just wasn't lucky. My supervisor, Ron Morrison, was going to jump across with me. It was very cold. The wind was gusting and the windchill was really low. I was nervous about jumping, but I trusted my boss completely. I'd been out to sea with him for about eight months and he was a very large and strong man. Ron put his arm around me and we jumped together. But when we jumped, a gust of wind threw us off balance and Ron and I went down between the two boats—they were only three feet apart—both of us bouncing like Ping-Pong balls against the sides of both ships. I hit the rub rail and broke my back in two places and cracked my head open. We hit the water like cement. What I remember is the lights on the boat. They were mint green as I started down into the depths. The deeper I went, the darker the lights became until there was nothing but blackness.

Back up on deck, Lane [Conway], who was deck boss on the *Constance,* dove into the water right after us. But the current was terrible and he couldn't see anything because of the foam from the engine overflow. He went down about five times looking for us and almost lost his life too on the last dive. He was just hanging on to the lower rail, gasping for air, thinking, "My god, they are really gone." Just as he started to climb over the top railing, he felt this unbelievable grip on the back of his left leg, then I came shooting up right next to him. I didn't know any of this at the time, but Ron had never let go of me. Somehow he got us up near the surface and then he threw me upward out of the water by my waist.

When I woke up I was on deck. John, the skipper of the *Constance,* who was a good friend, was leaning over me. He kept saying over and over, "I'd die if you died in front of me, Holly." I knew I was hurt but felt no pain. I was so cold, that's all I thought of.

No one knew what to do with me. While the men were all arguing over what they should do, a gal named Sebrina, who was the cook on the *Constance,* dragged me into the bathroom, sat me on the toilet, and just peeled my clothes off. She held me up in the shower and kept the water temperature cold and then gradually made it warmer and warmer until my body temperature came back closer to normal.

It was night so no planes could come to MedEvac me. I spent that night curled up in a bunk wrapped up like a mummy. I still didn't have any pain until I woke up a couple hours later. When I opened my eyes, the pain hit me like a huge wave. I was swollen up all over. My arms and thighs were so swollen I could hardly move, even breathe. My body hurt everywhere possible. They picked me up and got me out on deck and then onto a crane that swung me onto the dock. A plane came soon after, and I was MedEvacked to the emergency room at Kodiak hospital.

I was told a few times I'd be lucky if I ever walked again. That was a hard thing to deal with, but the more anyone says I can't, the hungrier I get. By the time I left the hospital, my doctor, Ron Brockman, had me walking out on one crutch. It took me a couple of years to get where I could walk and move around again. But it didn't stop me. And that's the part that I know I'm addicted to, you see. I was aware the whole time I was out fishing that I was risking my life. I never really slept. But the interest, the challenge of surviving, the thrill—I believe that's addictive. It's like a drug, as you know: look at all the men that keep doing it. We do it till we're fifty, till we fall apart. We're challenging her, the sea, is what we're doing. I know we're never going to win, but it's the competition that excites us. There's nothing that compares, not sex, nothing. It keeps your heart beating, your eyes sparkling; it keeps you alive inside. There's nothing like that, pulling away from the dock, leaving all those people on shore, the "nine-to-fivers" we called them, and not knowing an hour from then if we'd be alive or not. A lot of people stand back and say, "I wish I could do that," and of course they don't. But I dared to break the rules!

Peggy Smith

Peggy Smith navigates the streets of Kodiak behind the massive wheel of a ten-ton truck. It's not a startling sight. Peggy looks comfortable and competent because for her it's a pretty mundane job compared with winter crabbing in the Bering Sea. Like Laurie Knapp and Holly Berry, she was there during the deadliest years and seasons of the now legendary king crab boom of the seventies and early eighties. She was one of the first women to work on the crabbers and got her first jobs the only way a woman could during that time—as a cook for $100 a day. Later she moved on to deckwork and was one of the first women to be hired as a deckhand and receive equal shares with the male crew. She saw it all—the icings, the sinkings, the injuries, the scramble for survival suits. At thirty-five, she *married. Now with two young children, Ellie, six, and Daniel, three, her perspective has changed.*

I was never afraid when I started fishing. It still baffles me to this day why I wasn't. I guess it was because I'd never been on the ocean before. We almost sank my first trip out. The *Rough and Ready* was not a good boat then. At that time it was owned by the cannery and skippers would just take it over, so it wasn't taken care of. I remember that first trip the alarms went off and all the guys were running around. I looked down in the engine room and the floorboards were floating. I started thinking, "Well, I guess I better get a little excited." So naive. I was so naive. And after they got that under control, then I heard "Get the fire extinguisher!" All the electronics in the wheelhouse started on fire. I remember going, "Oh my gosh! My first trip out!" And I still went, and went again.

Later I went crabbing. My job was to sort the crab out on deck. You're kneeling down on the deck and you're bending over, too. That's what I did. One time we were fishing in really rough seas. The skipper was a real gung-ho guy. He wanted to do sixteen pots an hour, which was a spectacular amount. It was a real bad storm, but he never stopped. He didn't care. So we were still fishing and I was throwing undersized crab over and looking back toward the stern of the boat. I had the line in my arm to throw it over, then the guy behind me had the buoys, and he throws them over. We were just about to throw it over, and the skipper went through a wave that came up over the davit and hit me, and I hit the pot. It slapped me right down on the pot. I was down on my hands and knees and my glasses were gone—I can't see a thing without my glasses. They were smashed. The guy behind me almost washed overboard. The pot went floating over the deck; a couple of the guys almost got crushed by it. I got up and looked down at the deck and there was blood everywhere. Of course the skipper, he was a madman. We had about eleven pots left. He goes, "Put her inside! Let's finish the string!" I was bleeding like a pig. And two of the guys grabbed me and they took me inside and sat me down. I was bleeding so bad. They were just so wonderful. They laid me down on the couch in the galley and gave me towels and ice. They go, "Now don't look in the mirror Peg." And then they ran out to finish the string. I went, "Don't look in the mirror!?!" So I immediately go running to look in the mirror. Yes, it was scary! This piece of skin was hanging over. It was so close to my eye—I almost lost that eye. It broke two bones. The skipper came running down then and said, "You're not going to sue me are you?" I said, "No." I never even thought about it. For one thing, you were on tiptoes being a woman in the fishing world. If I had sued him, I would never have gotten another job. And that was the first thing I thought of.

We had to buck the storm all the way in to go to the doctor. It was real rough, so I was just trying to keep in the bunk, keep my face from hitting anything. I think I was in shock because I don't remember the pain at all. Not at all. The guys would come in and pack towels around me so I wouldn't roll. And they would bring me popsicles. Oh, they were so sweet. Every half hour here was a popsicle, 'cause it was the only thing I could keep down. The only medication—we had no medical kit—the only thing he had for pain was Empirin. And they have that codeine in them and my stomach couldn't handle it. That's all we had for pain pills. So for twenty-two hours into town they were up there with a popsicle or a new pack of ice for my face or a pain pill. All of them were just so sweet.

At that time, at Dutch Harbor all they had was a Vietnam medic. His name was Arnie or Ernie. That was their doctor. By the time we got in it was like twenty hours later. The skin had started growing already. He had to cut more away. For two and a half hours he worked on me doing intricate little stitches. He did a real good job. He said he'd had a lot of practice in 'Nam. I had forty-eight stitches.

The skipper was crazy, though. I was on the boat I think a month or two with him. We went through one green guy, if not two, every time we came to town, which was once every seven to ten days, depending on when we filled up. Sometimes it was only three days. But he was so insane. He would say, "Don't ever call me crazy!" That should have been my first indication—"Don't go on this boat, Peggy." You go on these boats and you think, "Okay, these guys can't handle it, but I'm going to handle it." I sort of knew about his reputation, but I had no idea it was going to be that bad. Truthfully I was kind of glad when I did have my accident. It was like a relief in a way.

So that same boat I was on, we were out during Thanksgiving in 1977, and I remember my turkey kept falling out of the oven it was so rough. Storms come up so fast out there. Within an hour you can go from five-foot seas to twenty-foot. This storm was outrageous. I'd say the waves were forty feet. I've had guys say they were eighty-feet big. We were a 110-foot boat and we looked like a little cork in the trough, the waves were so far above us. By then everybody had stopped fishing. We were jogging with it and we'd go down into the sea and both the waves behind you and in front of you would be above the boat completely.

We had two green guys on the boat. One of the green guys, a real young guy, just nineteen, was on wheelwatch and went to turn the boat. You usually try to keep it about four knots when you're doing this because the seas are so terrible. When you turn, you have to go a little bit faster, and this guy put it in full speed and turned it and we hit this wave that knocked our spinner window back twenty feet and imbedded the glass of that window into the shower. I was in the lounge and saw this thing go flying by, not knowing what it was. And then here's this water gushing down the stairs! The wave knocked the house back so you could see daylight. The water was just rushing in under the house of the boat. So I run in there and this boy is sitting in his underwear and his T-shirt still going full speed. We're headed ten knots into these waves and he's just dumbfounded. He doesn't know what to do. I start yelling, "Slow it down! Slow it down!" He finally pulled it back and there's glass and there's water, about seven inches, all over the wheelhouse. The skipper comes in and yells, "Turn it around!" and everybody's really getting excited. It was a frantic mess.

I ran down to the galley and I had the turkey for Thanksgiving in the oven. Well the turkey is out of the oven and I had to chase it around on the galley floor! But all our electronics were gone. Everything. We didn't have survival suits. This is before then. We did have a raft. But our pump still worked and our tanks were fine. We were not in danger so much of sinking, more in danger of getting lost, because all our electronics were out. We had a compass that could tell us which way town was, and that was about it. And we were way out—there's no land, no radar, nothing. That was a big, scary thing. We had to jog into town. It took us about twenty hours to get in. That was one of the first times I was really scared.

They used to put green guys on wheelwatch all the time. I used to go up with a real green guy. I'd say, "I know I'm a woman, and men don't like to take any instructions from women, but I just want you to know, this is the gyro, this is the automatic pilot, this is the . . ." And I'd try to go over everything because the skippers just got so tired of doing that that they didn't. They wouldn't. They'd say, "We're going from A to B, wake me up in two hours." I'd tell them, "You've got to look outside because our tanks should always be flowing. You've always got to check the tanks to make sure the pump hasn't stopped, because that's the first thing that makes a boat go down." I'd tell them to always go down in the engine room and check the floorboards, make sure they're not floating. I learned that on another boat.

I didn't care if the skipper knew I was doing this or not. And I'd try to be real delicate with them because, of course, they didn't want to take anything from any woman. But because a lot of them were green and scared, they wanted to know.

I've seen a lot of guys wash around on deck. I saw a guy break a couple of ribs. He got stuck between the cod end [the part of the trawl net that holds the fish], which is like forty-five tons, and the boat. He fell and the cod end shifted and just squished him. The worst thing with guys, though, is a toothache. I've seen guys handle a broken arm better than an abscessed tooth. And the skipper won't haul them into town for a toothache, not even for a broken arm. I remember, we had a few green guys who were so seasick they locked themselves in the stateroom because the skipper wanted them out on deck—he didn't care. There was this one guy who was sick for days. I went in and said, "You've got to eat something." He was totally dehydrated and had turned yellow. He was delirious—I think he was dying. I made him drink chicken broth. And he was just like a little boy. I think he was calling me Mom there for awhile. Oh gosh, it was just terrible. And I'd have to knock and go, "It's me," 'cause they wouldn't open the door for fear it was the skipper.

The worst experience I ever had was when we were dragging with the *Alert*. It was January, February, down at the south end of Kodiak Island. We were joint venturing with the Japanese. A big storm came up and we were icing up bad. It must have been blowing eighty to one hundred knots. It was just incredible. We'd chip ice with the baseball bats. Always the bats. It would be six inches deep after a couple of hours. Then we'd go out and chip more ice; come in, get warm, go out, chip ice. It was just terrible. It was so scary. We had already delivered our fish and decided to jog into Bumble Bay for protection. The *Alert* headed for the mainland. I still don't know why they did that. Well, it was closer, for one. We were real close to the mainland, but there was a westerly going right over those glaciers, just instant freeze on us. So we went with it, into Bumble Bay. And we're talking to the *Alert* the whole time. I was up there with the skipper; we're all talking to the *Alert*. They were going to turn and come our way and then that was it. Never heard from them again. It was spooky. They never found a thing. They just iced up so bad they turned right over and sunk.

I went downstairs saying to myself, "It's okay Peg, everything's okay." And then I saw my skipper's got his survival suit out of the bag ready to put on. And everyone else thinks everything's fine. I decided to get *my* survival suit on. Well, come to find out, these survival suits haven't been out of their sacks for years. None of the zippers work. They're all rusted. Nobody has waxed a zipper in years. The guys are still telling me that everything's okay while I'm working away at my zipper! From then on, every time I stepped on a boat I went and checked the survival suits, waxed the zippers, made sure they were okay. Survival suits used to be the last thing you could find in the bottom of a closet. The creases from the suits being folded up can cause leaks. You can't get the zippers up. They used to give plastic whistles that when they get wet don't do anything. It was just incredible. It used to be that way. Not so much anymore. But that was my scariest time.

I loved it, though. I think most of it was the money behind it all and the excitement, the excitement of survival. A lot of the women I met in fishing were thrill-seeking women, women who weren't afraid to do something out of the ordinary, have a good time. And I really enjoyed working with men, too. I grew up on a farm and always worked with my dad and three brothers.

But when I think about it now, I think, "You were crazy! You were crazy!" I wouldn't do it now. But see, children have really changed my life. I don't go out on these thrill-seeking adventures anymore. I don't even like getting into a 747 with my children, you know? Now it's all so different after I had my kids.

My mother couldn't believe it when I started working on a boat. My father passed away when I was sixteen. He never got to see me in this. But my mother, of course, she was shocked. And now that I've had a daughter, you know, my mom said, "Well, what will you think when Ellie goes fishing?" I said, "Well, she'll go fishing on our salmon fishing boat, but she will never go out to the Bering Sea." Because I will not allow her to!

Debra Nielsen

After being skiffman with her partner, Red, and running her own boat, Debra knows the statistics and many of the faces behind them. Red was one of them. She nearly was another. Although it's been six years since the sinking of the Wayward Wind, *we both sat through tears as Debbie recounted the events of that January night on the south end of Kodiak. The price she has paid for choosing this occupation has been high, she acknowledges, but she still finds commercial fishing "a worthwhile endeavor."*

When we were fishing on the south end [of Kodiak Island] and the boat sank, I saw the final conclusion that some fishermen see, because I was in the water for six hours in a survival suit. The boat sank when we had five skippers on board. And I think that's something people need to know. We were all friends for almost twenty years. Everybody on board had a lot of knowledge. But one thing was overlooked: we were pumping on our crab and the hatch cover wasn't put down properly on the stern. Because everybody was a skipper, nobody was checking each other's work. Red and I went to sleep. When we woke up the entire stern was underwater. The man on the wheel just didn't feel it settling because he was bucking into it. He apparently didn't think anything was wrong and obviously didn't get up to check the vessel in his watch. But it's a lesson in complacency. When people get to a certain level of knowledge you can think you've got it, but you still have to go through every routine, every single small detail still has to be checked. And that one was just a clear error that was too late to rectify.

We had about five minutes to get into survival suits. And that's something people don't think about when donning survival suits: you're pitching the whole time, so you're actually being thrown from side to side. This was January, so you always have some seas. It wasn't terribly rough, but rough enough where you were feeling the waves. Probably about fourteen-foot seas, maybe. We were being thrown to the deck when we were trying to put the suits on. And then when we got out to the bow, I asked if anyone had a line, and no one had a line. So we got a line from underneath our feet to try to hold onto. I didn't know where Red was. It turns out he was in the engine room still trying to save the boat. Even though the boat was going down he was trying to do something.

The wind was just roaring. The water at that point was about halfway up the stern. It was starting to sink pretty quickly and no one had the EPIRB, that's a locating beacon that the Coast Guard can pick up when people go into the water. So I went back inside the boat to get the EPIRB. And when I got back out onto the bow, I tried to give it to one of the guys beside me. It's large; it's probably six inches in diameter, and maybe about fourteen inches high and a little bit heavy. I'm five feet tall and weigh one hundred pounds. I was wearing a large suit, big mitts, and I didn't think I could hang onto it when I got thrown into the water. So I tried to hand it to the guy next to me. I wasn't sure who it was because he was in the survival suit too and I couldn't tell. But he asked me what it was when I started to hand it to him. I said, "It's an EPIRB." He said, "A what?" Apparently he was the only person on board who wasn't a skipper, who wasn't familiar with it. I took it back, and I thought, "I've got to hang onto this." So when we got thrown into the water, I had the EPIRB in my hands and I had the rope in my hands. I got thrown in a somersault backwards. I couldn't protect myself because my hands were full. I hit my head on the hull but not real hard, just pretty hard, and then my shoulder. I still had hold of the EPIRB though. I can just remember underwater thinking, "I've got to hang onto this, that's all that's important."

Finally I got away from the hull, kicked out, and the first thing I saw was a trailer buoy, a little white trailer buoy. I grabbed hold of that too because immediately when I got in I couldn't get my head to stay up. These suits had a little inflatable neck support that keeps your head up so you don't drown. It's kind of like a tire where you have to push in the little button and blow. That's a really awkward thing to do in the water when you've got waves throwing you around, but it's really critical to get that blown up. They now have automatic ones that blow up instantly with little CO_2s [carbon dioxide cartridges]. I couldn't get the nozzle in my teeth to press it and blow it up and breathe because my head was going underwater. I had both hands on the EPIRB and I was just being thrown around. If I hadn't found that buoy I would have died. I was just lucky and grabbed it and stuck it behind my head. And that's what held me up all night was the buoy behind my head.

I still had to get the EPIRB on somehow, though. I had these big floppy gloves. The little toggle switch On was so tiny that it's like a design flaw for that particular model. Remember this was all stuff that was just coming out the time this happened, in 1987. Since then they've done some other things, like have them be water activated so they come on automatically.

I drifted into somebody and I told them to hang onto me 'cause I had the EPIRB. He hung onto me. We drifted into somebody else and I told him to hang onto me, that I had the EPIRB, but he didn't, and I couldn't hang onto him because I was holding onto the EPIRB. He just drifted off, I think maybe because he was in shock. But the other people apparently didn't hold onto the line when they went off the boat because some time during the night I yelled to the person next to me, "Pull in the line! I want to make sure everybody's there!" You had to shout because these big combers would come. He pulled in the line, and there wasn't anybody at the end of the line. Then I knew they were gone. I kept thinking, though, if I could get the EPIRB turned on that maybe they'd still find everyone because we were all in the same place and we had gotten a Mayday out. We were clear on the south end of Kodiak Island, really a long way from town.

It was night, it was snowing, it was January. So I remember lying in the water and looking up and seeing seagulls flying over my head and the snow coming down. It was just beautiful, really really beautiful. And it was so cold. I started feeling really tired. I kept thinking, "I'll just rest for a little while, then I'll try again." Then I'd think, "No, no, don't rest. If you rest, you're going to go to sleep and then you'll die. And if you die everybody's going to die because you've got the EPIRB." And I think knowing you're the one who's got the keys to everybody else living is what gives you that incentive to try harder and try harder. So I kept trying to find that little switch. I was lying on my back in the waves. You could hear the waves coming and you could brace for them, but then I'd have to get the buoy back underneath my neck again after each wave.

We were probably in the water two or three hours before I finally thought I got it. I could feel something and then I could see a light, so then I knew I had it. As soon as I had it I said to the person next to me in the water, "I got it! I think I got it!" He said, "Well, turn it off again and then try turning it on again to make sure you have it." I thought, "No." I didn't touch it again. I just left it and I held onto it and it was on.

By that time we were getting really weak and cold. Water was running into the survival suit through the sides and the back. I was starting to get hypothermic. The man who was next to me kept trying to hold me up. He would put his arm around me to hold me up. At one time I remember I tied the EPIRB to him because I thought I was going to die and I didn't want him to get lost. I thought, "He'll live longer, his suit fits him better." So I was tying it to him kind of around his leg and here and there, and he said, "What are you doing?" And this kind of made me laugh even then because it was such a funny sound in his voice, like "What are you mauling me for?" I said, "I'm tying the EPIRB to you in case I can't hang onto you anymore."

About three hours later I heard a helicopter. When they came over to us, and I knew they had located us, I just had this feeling like "Just another adventure. They'll find everybody. Just one of those deals. We lost the boat, Oh well!" But I had no doubt because they had found us that they would find everybody else and it was all fine, that it was going to be fine. Then they lowered the basket. I thought the worst was over until I tried to get into the basket. In those kind of seas with the helicopter above just trying to keep it near you . . . We swam for the basket. At that point Jay, the man in the water with me, tried to grab it. Of course that's an incredible force, but he was trying to grab it and grab me and get me into the basket before he got in. He hurt his arm doing it. I knew when it swung by again I better get in because he wasn't going to get into the basket until I got in the basket. So I swam as fast as I could and got in. That protective quality I was talking about, I really admire it in men. It's a wonderful trait. They jerked the basket up and dropped it back for Jay and he got in.

The Coast Guard then took us to a remote site where they fuel on Sitkinak Island. We were there when they told us that they had found the others but that they were dead. So there were four people who died and two who lived. They were really well-known people, people that everyone missed very much and the town really felt that loss. We know how valued these people were, people who take up a lot of space. You can't fill that space with anybody else.

Afterwards, even with all the death and all the pain, I wanted people to know that what they're doing really matters. I would never say about fishing that it isn't worth it. It *is* worth it, even if you lose the person you love the most or your own life doing it. It's a worthwhile endeavor because it's everything you are. We never feel truly alive unless we do the things in our lives that take the measure of everything we are, the depth and breadth and width and heighth of us. We will always feel cheated, we will always feel like we're not quite getting there. We will always feel dismayed with our own abilities if we don't really reach those perimeters of ourselves. And fishing takes you there. It doesn't give you a choice. It's life itself. I think that there are very few enterprises in life where you meet those horizons on a daily level. You see them once in a while and it makes a story, but in fishing every day's a story. Every moment practically is a story. Something new is always happening because nature is changing around you all the time. You've got to rise and fall at her level and her demand and figure out a scenario where you're going to keep yourself and your crew safe and perform a skill within the framework that nature's presented to you at that moment.

People who are doing this particular profession, they know what they're doing. They know how high the stakes are, and they do know it's worth it. It isn't about money. It truly is about skills and about living in an incredible environment and about learning the depth of who you are. And I think that's something that the marketing, the politics, the cost of the vessels and the gear—it's taken away from what people really came here to do. I think it's those realities we need to be reminded of, that if you wouldn't do it as a lifestyle, you probably shouldn't do it. Because otherwise it isn't worth it. So go do something else. It really does have to be who you are should the stakes be as high as what I had to pay.

6 *"If I'm Still Fishing . . ."*

JUNE 9, 1982, BEAR ISLAND

I'm not going out with the men tonight to put out the nets. I am relieved, but I feel guilty. It is blowing, as it always seems to on put-out nights. I suppose I will get over this, walking to the window every few minutes, looking out wondering what they are doing out there, feeling as though I should be helping. But I have to say put-outs are the worst, and I'm glad to be on shore. Overall I have such a sense of relief about the summer before me. No more full-time in the skiff! Now I can be a human being again.

*T*he first year I fished, I wore a pagouk hat like my husband; I wore the same black hip boots, the same Helly Hansen rain gear. Striding up the beach to an annual fisherman's picnic on the Fourth of July, a neighboring fisherman commented, "Leslie, you look just like the crew." I felt that way too. I absorbed, embraced that identification. I felt completely submerged by this new life and this new place that was so much larger and greater than anything I had previously known. I lost myself in it, in belonging to it the only way you could—by throwing yourself into the boat at all hours and giving your life over to the fish, the fish, the fish that never stopped filling the nets. And the nets that always needed mending, mending.

I am not that same person. I have laid down the rain gear and the pagouk hat. Some years I bought my own rain gear, wore my own versions of fishing hats and skiff gear. But mostly I gradually stepped out of the obsessiveness that is needed to make a fishing operation work. At the time, it seemed a luxury for me to do this, and it was only possible by hiring a crewman to replace me. But it was also a necessity. Parts of me were dying, but not just my joints and back. I could not survive more than five years with such singular attention to this work whose monotony and tyranny shut out other parts of my being: the student, the teacher, the writer, the reader, the contemplative and spiritual self. And then there was our marriage. In calmer moments, when the nets slowed their silent snagging of salmon, we both realized there was something much larger at stake than how many fish we would catch that day. And so I "retired." I did not step out of fishing altogether, though. I was "auxiliary," the backup, the extra crew in times of blows, when nets were taken up or put out, when an extra set of hands was needed to help relieve other, exhausted hands. That role I loved and could do. And so it continued until the arrival of children. We are expecting the fourth this year; it will be born smack in the middle of the fishing season.

This, then, is my abbreviated story of "If I'm Still Fishing . . ." the words Lisa Jakubowski used to describe her ambivalent determination to leave the industry. Looking ahead instead of behind and around, I am asking where do fishing women envision themselves beyond this season and the next? How sustainable is each woman's presence in an industry fraught with risk, harassment, uncertainty, compromise? I am not asking the larger question of the future of women in the fisheries. It is an individual question: Where do you want to be five years from now? Are you "in" or "out" and for how long? For me, I am both "in" and "out" and I am both for the rest of my life. For better or worse, I will be involved in commercial fishing until the salmon stop returning to their streams. It is the heritage I have wed and am even now still making my own.

I know other women whose stories are like mine. Sandy Earle is one. She fishes across the bay from us; she too is both "in" and "out," and for some of the same reasons. Lisa Jakubowski, after ten intensive years of commercial fishing, says she is definitely "out"—maybe. Laurie Jolly and Rebecque Raigoza, after two fishing seasons, are both enthusiastically "in"—for life, they hope. Lori Francisco Johanson and Terri Francisco Barber, sisters who grew up salmon fishing, are both trying to find ways to keep on fishing, to "stay in" despite changing life circumstances.

For every woman who fishes, who has ever fished, there is a story of circumstances and motivations that result in the decision to come or go or to compromise on a third, uneasier choice, as I have done. Not every woman feels such control over her life, however. One woman I interviewed told of helplessness and embitterment. In middle age, she had married a fisherman and only found out afterward that she was expected to work with him on the boat during the summers. She was given no choice, and though twelve seasons have passed, all twelve of them in long, wearying work in fishing, she has still been unsuccessful in forging a compromise with her husband. I fear and ache for her, but I can do nothing to help. Every woman must pioneer her own way, both in and out of this life called fishing.

Laurie Jolly and Rebecque Raigoza

When I met with Laurie and Rebecque they exuded energy and enthusiasm about their beach seining operation and felt they had found their future here in Alaska.

Rebecque: Alaska for me was like a fantasy thing. You hear about it, you watch Alaska on TV, about making your fortune in Alaska, and I did it! I'm here. I've done it. I can go back and I can show other people. I was with a youth group of like thirty students to Africa this past month and I was telling a lot of the girls, "Yeah, I fish in Alaska," and I was sharing all my stories and all my fears with them and all the things I've accomplished, all the strength I feel. A lot of them were like, "Wow! That's what I want to do." I feel as long as I share myself and my experiences with other people, more women will become involved and interested in it.

Laurie: Being out here has definitely changed me. It's just so easy in the artificial world that some people call the real world to just fall into the nine-to-five and lose yourself. Up here I feel like I have myself. No matter what happens, I'm the only person that I can answer to. Sometimes when I'm down there I have a hard time with that. I just don't want to see what's happened to my mom and other women; I don't want that for me—just the housewife. I want to have an identity. I want people to know me as Laurie Jolly. I don't want people to say, "Oh, there's Brian's girlfriend." I want to be somebody, somebody who is strong, and I can feel good about what I am doing. I'm not hurting anyone else by fishing. It's kind of a down-to-earth way of living, real basic.

We try not to hurt the environment. Although I do feel kind of sorry for the salmon but I figure that Fish and Game does such a good job with regulation. I used to be a hard-core vegetarian. I wouldn't eat fish or anything, so sometimes I have a hard time with that, the whole sense of killing. But that was overcome because I've always enjoyed fishing. And I know that the fish are going to be enjoyed. The other day I killed a silver that was really nice. I felt kind of bad for it, but I appreciate that I got it.

Eventually I'd like to see if I could get a beach seine permit myself. I guess you have to fish for three years. But even then I don't know if I would be comfortable getting a permit after next season. I think I have to learn a little bit more. Fifteen years from now I would hope to be a permit holder. And I would definitely consider myself a fisher, because right now I want to do that. This year has made such a difference. I also think about having a setnet site, but I really enjoy beach seining. There are so many things you have to know about the wind and the currents and the tide and everything. They can just take your seine away, collapse it. There are a lot of dangers.

Rebecque: I'm the type of person who would rather not know what the dangers are. My parents say to me, "There are bears out there. You'll get eaten alive!" Men tell me, "You don't want to get a job beach seining. This can go wrong, that can go wrong. I knew this guy, this happened to him . . ." I don't want to hear about any of that. I'm just going to be with responsible people, try to be as observant as I can. I wouldn't stay in a situation that was too much for me to handle. When dangerous things come up, you just do the best you can.

Coming out here and finding my independence and strength, I don't get that back home in the city working in a photo lab or working in a restaurant driving a car around town and dealing with materialism and smog and traffic and crime and all that. Out here there's freedom and the land and there's friendly people and a good person to work with. You're feeling physically well and mentally well because you know you can do the job. It's so rewarding.

I developed such a sense of independence and strength. Things I thought I could never do I learned I could do out here. It's just opened a whole new world for myself as a young woman, becoming a woman, I don't know. There are so many possibilities now because I know that I can do "a man's job," you know? There's a lot of power that comes from that.

It even opens doors when I'm back at home. Maybe I could find myself doing something I wouldn't have thought I could have done before. Any of those things I know I can do. I know because I've challenged myself out here and I've succeeded as far as I'm concerned.

Another factor for coming back is seeing the women that I've met. Jan [Axel] for one. She just possesses a power that I want to take ahold of. She's self-supporting, she's a wonderful woman. She seems fulfilled. She's making money. She's got a business in Kodiak. She built her own home. She has a setnet site. People love her, they respect and admire her—I want that! She's incredible.

It's fun, because I feel like a bond immediately with other women that are fishing. It's like all of sudden I feel a sense of friendship and community.

Laurie: Last summer, I was talking to another kid who had come up, and we were just talking about how when you come up to Alaska, everything works out. It's like a magical place. One minute everything's going wrong, then the next, everything's good. I don't know why, but I think it's fate or destiny. Alaska is just a special place.

Rebecque: The people make it special. It's a small community out here. People are closer, word of mouth goes faster. That's what I think. You just meet good people. The first step is getting lucky and meeting a good person. And that's not hard. There are lots of good people. You work hard and do your best and people are going to see it. Honest to goodness, it works here.

Sandy Earle

Sandy's history in fishing goes back twenty-five years to the late sixties when she and her husband, Danny, came adventuring to Alaska. That first year they leased Dora Aga's setnet site off Kodiak Island. Left with out-dated gear and few instructions, they had every reason to quit, but didn't. They kept at it, trying out different fisheries until 1975, when they were able to buy their own setnet permit. After a number of years in the skiff, Sandy decided it was not a part she could continue. She is still an integral part of the fishing operation, but she works primarily on shore.

Those early years fishing with Danny were tumultuous. We would just get so frustrated with the gear and our lack of knowledge to make things right or easy. And the tides would run horribly there. The corks would pop off the net and the net would be flying on top of the water. We would be out there at a loss as to how to cope. We shouldn't even have tried, but we would try to fight it. We would have to pull so hard on the lines, my arms were being pulled out of the socket. It did get better eventually. We got better gear. And Danny came to understand my limitations more, that there were certain things I couldn't do.

Our relationship was much different on shore. There wasn't all the tension of having to do something right then or that the set was coming apart. But I'd have to stand at the sink all day doing dishes after having been out fishing so much. I found myself becoming exhausted, mentally and physically, by the whole thing. Staying up late at night trying to get things done. And sometimes Danny would go out very early in the morning by himself because I could not get up. But I think he started realizing that I had just had it. At that point we realized he needed a crew member if we wanted to start catching more fish. And relations weren't so great between us then.

Mark was our first crewman. That first year was really difficult for me. I was being usurped. My identity was being taken away from me. It was a mutual decision, but when it actually came down to it, they'd get ready to go and do this exciting work, and this work that made money and contributed, and the attitude was, "Well, you can stay home and cook, and we'll be back in a few hours and we'll have lunch when we get back." Here I was with a pile of dishes and a house to clean. I really was angry a lot that summer. I really resented not Mark, but having my position taken away from me because my identity was all tied up with that. And I talked about it with some friends. One in particular said, "I like staying at home. It's nice not having to put on the slimy rain gear, cold gloves all hours of the day and have your day interrupted constantly." It took me a summer to get over that. I went out some of the time, maybe once a day, or the whole day sometimes. It wasn't an immediate cutting off point; it was gradual.

After that we hired two other people. Then I was back to being a full-time crew member again to have an even number, two skiffs. That went on for another four years. I always fished with Dan. There were times I would run the skiff, so I felt competent about that except one time.

There was a terrible southwest swell coming in. It was one of the worst I've ever seen. Danny and Alex went out to pick one net, and Mark and David and I picked the inside net, which wasn't quite so bad. We picked the net and the wind was picking up the whole time. By the time we got to the end of the net, I thought, "This is really bad. We shouldn't be out here." But Danny and Alex were still at the other net. I thought—probably a bad judgment call on my part—but I thought we had better go help.

We were coming from our net, and we would be down in these swells and you couldn't see anything else. And then we'd go back up. When we were going back up, the bow of the skiff was way out of the water and then it would go back down and we couldn't see anything. Probably ten- to twelve-foot swells. I was running the motor because I was the skipper that time. I sort of got mesmerized by the whole thing. Instead of using good judgment and saying, "They can handle it, but we're not going to do any good out there" and coming in to the cove, I just felt we had this obligation to check them out.

The further we got out there, the bigger the swells got. I have this picture in my mind of getting close to the net and seeing Danny and Alex up on the peak of a wave. Their bow was out of the water, the stern was out of the water, and they were just sort of up on the peak of a wave. That's when panic set in and I just sort of kept going. I didn't know what to do. It was too nasty to turn around. I was terrified of getting sideways in the swell. Finally we got close to the net and pretty close to their skiff and Danny just yelled, "Get out of here!" 'cause we could have just slammed right into them. I didn't know how to get out of there! I was stuck out there. The only thing I could think of was, "Keep your bow into it." But the bow was going where I didn't want to go. I just turned to Mark and said, "Help!" He got us turned around. He said, "I thought you were doing fine." I said, "I was terrified." He said, "But you had a smile on your face." I said, "I do that when I'm terrified." So now he knows never to trust me when I'm smiling in the skiff.

But we got back and Danny said, "That was really stupid of you to come out there." I said, "Yeah, I knew once I got out there." That made me realize that if Mark hadn't been there, it would have just been me and David, and David was just here for a vacation. I thought, "I had their lives in my hands. What if something had happened?" I had a horrible two or three weeks thinking about that, what could have happened. After that it really shook my confidence in my judgment. I thought, "I really don't want to be out there." I just started to realize that maybe it was time to settle down and stay home and find other things to do.

That was a bit of a turning point. I still have that silhouetted in my mind. Danny had been subtly pushing me that way. I think he was relieved. There were always times I would say, "Why can't we do it this way or that way?" I was always looking for an easier way to do things. So I think he was relieved to be the only voice in the skiff and things went much easier on shore. Meals were more regular, the house was cleaner, clothes got washed, and business things were taken care of. Things just went a lot smoother. We got along better because we didn't carry those things on shore.

Things are much better now. We're much more efficient, things are running smoother. I'm much happier. The few times I do go out now, I look back and think, "I just don't know how I put up with the constant interruptions before, the coming in, the eating, the going back out again three times a day." Our schedule went something like this. Get up at 6:30 or 7:00. Be out by 7:00 or 7:30. Go out until 11:00 or 12:00. Come back in, eat sort of a breakfast, a big heavy breakfast. And immediately I would be overcome with the urge to sleep. I remember a few mornings when I was still eating and Danny would have his boots on: "Okay, let's go!" The dishes were still on the table, food needed to be put away. I remember that horrible feeling: "Oh no, got to do it again!" We'd go back out for a shorter pick, then come back in, make dinner, eat dinner, just put the dishes in the sink, go out again for the evening pick, come back, and be faced with a pile of dirty dishes. Invariably I'd say, "I'll do them tomorrow." In the morning would start the same thing. The dishes would pile up and finally I would find some energy to do them, like late at night. Then I would collapse and start over the next day. This was in my heyday, when I was a crew member and was depended upon.

Also we would go out and it would be really rough. Swells would be big. I'd get seasick. Then I was useless and Danny would be having to work twice as hard in horrible weather. I felt like a slacker but there were times I just couldn't work anymore.

I don't know physically how much longer I could have held out. When we first started fishing and when I did it all the time, I would get tired and exhausted, but it was a good exhaustion, the exhaustion of accomplishment. I was doing it constantly so I was in better shape. My arms were stronger. I never had back problems, although almost everyone else seemed to. But now I do have back problems and I'm not even fishing. It was just draining. Just the constant going, you're constantly going. Constantly physically alert. When it's rough out there you have to watch yourself. You can get hurt, you can fall down. It's just hard, demanding on your body.

There's a pride you take in doing that work, but then you see your body being abused. I would look at some people in Larsen Bay, and I don't know what their other circumstances were, but they had been setnetting all their life and they had a lot of physical problems. It was a self-realization thing, that this is my only body and I'm going to need it when I'm older too. I don't want to wear out before my time.

I've realized now how important it is to make it easier for Danny to go out there. I know it's not a picnic out there; it's no fun. He still gets enjoyment out of it, but he's getting older. He needs just as much coddling as I do and did to make his job easier. I still admire him for getting up and doing it day in, day out. I feel very fortunate because I have a lot more free time than he does. I feel sometimes guilty because I waste a lot of it doing my own thing. When I'm doing something completely for myself, or when I'm not going out, I still feel guilty about them. I feel like I'm sending them out to support my lifestyle. I feel guilty about that especially when the weather's bad, but that's the arrangement. I do my part here, but it's easy compared to what they're doing. But it is necessary. That's always what I have to remind myself.

Lori Francisco Johanson and Terri Francisco Barber

From my island, I can see across the water to the Franciscos' fish camp, to its warehouses, cabins, and meticulous grounds. I have clear memories of the family as they were when I first came to Uyak Bay, especially of the two girls and two boys ranging from fifteen to eight years old who were as adept and proficient at running skiffs and picking fish as any adult out there. Eighteen years later, they all still come back, interrupting their lives Outside to do what they have done all their lives—setnetting for salmon. For Lori and Terri the annual return is no longer easy. Both are married, both have an infant, a toddler, and a preschooler, both have husbands who cannot leave their jobs. Still, the two women have returned and have continued to fish through their separations from their husbands, through pregnancies, through nursing babies. This interview took place in the middle of the salmon season, after we all had been fishing for more than thirty days without a break. Terri was then five months pregnant.

Lori: We could go way back and say our family first began fishing over across the bay at Greenbanks.

Terri: Was I two then? But we didn't actually start helping out till we were ten, eleven. We just had that one set, right? I remember Lori going out there with Dad sometimes 'cause she was the oldest.

Lori: We just had one big set, and then I don't know how many years later we had another smaller net. So we started off small and gradually grew bigger. We had one skiff, a wooden boat. Actually Dad went out a lot by himself. We remember lying in bed at night listening to him go by.

Terri: Wasn't that like when we set out at midnight? Didn't we do that for a while? And I remember Lori comforting Mom, like Mom would lie there in bed all worried at night, and Lori would say, "It's okay Mom, it's okay." It's pitch black. It's hard to believe they did it like that back then. Out there all by himself.

Lori: Tim [older brother] and I would go out more often than Terri and Bryan [younger brother] did back then. We would go out, we wouldn't necessarily work. I remember a lot of times just sitting in the back of the boat watching Dad. He would pick over the bow. We'd count fish or whatever. We helped. Then later on, I remember Terri and I going out together more so than we do nowadays. We normally don't go out together nowadays. But I remember Terri and I together. We started running boats young.

Terri: Remember when you wrote that article for *Alaska Magazine*? You were running boats then. You were twelve.

Lori: Yeah, we were pretty young.

Terri: I don't think we really were conscious of being so young and being the only girls fishing. I am more so these days. I was telling Lori, we were just talking about fishing, and I said, I think it's pretty neat. Now there are more and more women, but when we were the only ones, I thought, "Wow, this is pretty neat." And we were so small. You grew up doing it; it was something you did, and we didn't think of it as anything special.

Lori: And I remember when we first had the T set, and that's our farthest net down. I remember when we first started to go down there, just us kids, we'd bring the walkie-talkie, tell Mom and Dad when we got down there. That was a big adventure. I remember them being a little nervous. That was when Dad didn't even come out with us then. He'd stay and we'd go by ourselves. And I remember being a little nervous. We ran the boat, did the whole thing all by ourselves. That was when we were in our teens. We got used to it pretty quick. Like you say, I don't think we thought about it back then. Maybe when we were in high school we were more conscious of it. There were very few female fishermen.

Terri: I don't really know a family like ours. We've always really gotten along so well because we were all each other had out here in the summers, in the winters, in the springtime. We were each other's best friends. We didn't have any other choice. And so we just really grew up that way. Not to say we didn't have any arguments, like all brothers and sisters do, but I don't remember any real fights.

Lori: Yeah, we'd just do the work together. No one person is any higher than the other.

Terri: Whoever got back there [in the skiff] first would get the engine down and drive.

Lori: I think back then I was more afraid than I am nowadays. Our equipment is better, we have the aluminum boats now, and that takes some of the fear out of things.

Terri: Well, if you're not driving. I can have so much confidence myself, but whoever's at the engine, really, that's a hard job. I like going with Bryan.

Lori: If we're supposed to sound like tough women, then . . .

Terri: I'd rather have someone else drive.

Lori: But we're totally capable. Sometimes we sit back and let them do the work.

Terri: Especially now that we're older and we're coming out here and we're pregnant, and . . . then it's let them drive, let them take the bow. We're really not out to prove anything, like maybe we used to be.

Lori: Yeah, "I'm tough, I can do it." The guys are a little stronger, let them handle the harder work. We didn't grow up thinking we had to prove anything. Maybe when we had helpers, when we hired crewmen, and we had to show them the ropes. If they couldn't handle something then we would jump right in and take over. We definitely still do that, even up till last year when we had crew. Many of the guys we've hired are just not cut out for this kind of work. I feel, I'm sure we all feel we're so much better at it than they are. This is our life, and we grew up doing this. We know our job; we know how it's done; this is what we do.

You know I think it's odd how so many people back in Maryland or wherever I go back home to during the winter just assume that I don't fish. They assume I come out here and, I don't know, cook, whatever.

Terri: They all do that: "What do *you* do out there?" I say, "The same thing my dad and my brothers do." Or they say, "Oh I can just see you on the beach with your fishing pole!" And I say, "No, It's not that kind of fishing." Yeah, they just have no clue.

Lori: I know this might sound strange, but I like the exercise in the fishing. Terri and I didn't fish as much last year with new babies. We had two crewmen to help; we really missed it a lot. There are times when you're out there on the water and you think, "Oh I wish I were at home right now, even doing dishes, something!" even though it's hard work to stay in camp too. But we really like the exercise. It's backbreaking work, yes, but it's good for you. I love it because it's family, it's the beauty, the money, yes!

Terri: I can be blunt about that. Besides what Lori said, on to the money thing. Sure, it's so hard leaving our husbands in the summer, especially now that we have babies and children, but by coming up here and fishing for three months in the summer then I can go back and have nine months and stay home with them. If I didn't come up here in the summer I would have to get a job and I'd have to put them in day care and I don't want to do that. We've always had Mom or Dad to stay home with us—us kids never went to day care. I just don't want to do that. Dan [husband] more or less told me, and I agree, that if I don't go up in the summers I would have to get a job, because it's hard to live off one income these days with a family, and so that's another thing that keeps us coming back is kids. I thought, "Well, when I have kids I'll stop coming up." But that's not right. And day care's so expensive these days, and I never did finish college. I don't have an education. What could I get—maybe a minimum wage job, a little better if I'm lucky. By the time you pay for a couple of kids in day care, you're just coming out even pretty much. That's what keeps me going through the summer. I think, "God, it's hard leaving Dan, especially now with kids." It's not fair to take the kids away from him, but it allows me to be home with them for nine months, and I wouldn't trade that for the world.

Lori: Yeah, exactly. I could teach during the year, but I want to stay with my children. I think that same thing, that same thought. I do this for three months and that's it. I don't have to work, can stay home with my kids.

Terri: It would be the ultimate for me, for my husband to be able to come and work with me. I know now, when I have another baby, you think, "Well, what if you have another kid? You have to draw the line somewhere. How much longer can I keep coming up?"

Lori: And Eric [husband] being a state trooper, he gets paid vacations. When he came up two summers ago, he took a leave of absence. They said they wouldn't entertain that idea again. So this summer, he's coming August 1 and staying until September 10. That's paid vacation, forty-five days' worth. So if he continues to save up sick days and holidays and all his vacations, then he will be able to take thirty days off a summer and do this, which we plan. I don't know how much longer I'll keep coming up, but we've also talked about doing something else so he could have his summers off. Something to talk about, think about.

Lori: Everything isn't always great in fishing. There are real miserable days when it's pouring down rain, you've got hair hanging down in your face, rain's dripping down. Nowadays I'm pretty dry, though. I've got my hair in a baseball cap. Even when we began we wore hip boots, then a long raincoat. And you would get wet, get your pants all gurry. Now it's nice pants, a jacket. Times have changed. The work is still pretty much the same, though.

Terri: I remember telling people it's so monotonous, so monotonous, but I haven't even thought about that this year. Funny, I don't know why, maybe I'm just getting used to it. We've done it for so long.

Lori: It's not that bad. By the very end, like the end of September, maybe. But like we say, it's so much easier nowadays. In the past it really got to us. It really got to me years ago when it seemed we were always out there and never on shore. But when you're always out there, then you're happy that you have all these fish. So you can't complain, even though it's back-breaking and you're exhausted at the end of the day. The other night I thought, I'm just going to fall into bed . . .

Terri: Lie there all night and count fish.

Lori: You see fish flash before your eyes.

Terri: I used to wake up at night dreaming, "No Terri, you can't lie down, you can't lie down." I'd wake up and be sitting up in bed tossing fish and counting them! It was awful. I remember sitting there talking, thinking, "What am I doing? Counting fish?"

Lori: There's going to come a day when I won't be coming back. I don't like to think about it. I always said a few years ago that I wanted to keep coming back for as long as I can.

Terri: I hate to deny my kids because we grew up doing this. My brother Bryan was telling me yesterday, he said, "Boy these years out here were some of the best years of my life." When he didn't have to fish, he'd sit down and build canneries. We'd be out here in the winters and ride Hondas on the beach. You really have to use your imagination out here. And I thought, I really don't want to deny my kids that. I'd love to keep bringing them up here for the summer. But what's fair?

Lori: I just remember growing up, being out here, thinking, "This is the greatest place there is," having the best time of my life. We loved coming out here. I remember that's why I wanted to be a teacher when I was young, so I could have my summers off so I could come back and fish. We don't really know what's going to happen now. It's scary.

Terri: I remember I couldn't wait for someone to take me away from all this! I couldn't wait to leave. Then I get married and I just keep coming back. That's why I think it's so funny.

Lisa Jakubowski

Lisa's experiences with harassment would seem enough justification for getting out, but she also names other concerns common to many women. Still, her determination to leave is matched only by the strength of her ambivalence.

When I first started fishing, I wanted to find my limits, but I was held back because of my seasickness. I didn't think I'd be wanted on one of those boats that really went for it. And last year, I got offered this really good job on this boat that really pushed to the limit. We stayed up for fifty hours, slept a couple hours, stayed up another fifty hours, slept another four, and went up for another fifty hours. I was hallucinating. It was ridiculous. There are much better ways to get work out of people. You can't use people like machinery. They're going to wear out. Then you're going to get less production out of them. Let people get some sleep, rotate someone in the bunk. When you get to the point of total exhaustion, you're going to need a lot more than two hours to get caught up.

The hallucination was really odd. It was night. I walked out on deck. I picked up what I thought was a little shore bird. I picked it up in my hands and am going, "Oh the poor little thing!" I'm looking at it for a good thirty seconds, and then I realized it was just a gill plate off a black cod. I threw it down and felt really creepy. It really freaked me out.

I also fell asleep at the coiler. My head was down; I was still moving. My eyes were closed I guess because they sent someone from the bait shed to wake me up. The next thing I know there's this guy standing in front of me. I said, "How did you get there?" I was in the middle of work.

I thought it was really dangerous. At that point, I thought, "I don't need this!" I'm thirty-one. I've had enough of pushing. I quit three times last season. But I'd always come back 'cause I'd forget. "Well," I'd say, "One more." I don't like to quit in the middle of a season. I think it was the crew that held me together. They were good people and I didn't want to let them down. I didn't want to give in either.

For those three trips I made about $9,000 for twenty-one days of fishing. It was worth it, but I wouldn't do it again. I had a miserable attitude. I hated myself, I hated everybody. When you're that tired, it's just horrible. I would get mad at the skipper in a way, but I'm for pushing hard. It was interesting to see how far I could be pushed. I had a good carrot to chase, though: I was doing it to get me through school. I kept saying to myself, "Now I know why I'm going to nursing school. That's right!" 'Cause I hate that sometimes too, but it's so much easier compared to longlining.

In '90 I had a job all lined up with someone I knew on a salmon boat. He made me commit till September or I'd be docked a percent. He called me two weeks before I was coming up and said he had bad news—I couldn't work for him. We had arranged this back in January! He said his partner's wife was jealous so I couldn't work on the boat. I don't even know his partner's wife. I was out of the job two weeks before it was supposed to start. I was infuriated, pissed! It was a friend also, but the friendship died because of it. I told the guy I thought this was really in poor taste. It was a business deal on his part. So I had to come up here and scrounge up jobs, which was difficult.

I ended up working for five people in four months, but I got lots of variety. I went out West longlining, did a little seining, driving a skiff. Then I got on the setnet site. That's what made things so hard. It's like a yo-yo not knowing what to expect. How this crew's going to react to me, how I'm going to . . . I felt like I had to please them. What does this crew want out of me?

So there have been a lot of ups and downs over the years. I've wanted to get out of fishing since '88. I bought a house in Bellingham [Washington] and thought I was going to work that winter and in the summer get a little nest egg and go back and just settle down. First that winter I got harassed so badly, then the oil spill—I thought, "Damn! What am I supposed to do?" But then I set a new goal of massage school. Fishing became then a means to education, to getting out of it. But the horrible thing is since '89 things have gotten better. I've been getting better jobs. It's like, "I'm getting out of this. I don't want these better jobs."

I finished massage school in '91 and needed to make some money, so I came up in March and walked the docks again. Then I really felt like I had to sell myself. I was really in debt. I went herring fishing in Cook inlet, then salmon. It was '91 when the price was half of what it used to be. I was working with young punks that drove me crazy. In fact we almost got in a fisticuff. Kind of a screaming match. I had just had it. We had untied from the dock one day at 11:00 A.M. The kid was drunk when we were leaving. I wasn't pleased about that. He just wasn't doing the normal things, picking up lines when you untie them, putting them away, making sure everything's squared away. I was driving the skiff—he wouldn't hook the skiff up. Like a really important part of the set. You want to get your skiff hooked up so you're ready to set again. He'd do everything but hook me up. I don't think he liked me. But he let it interfere with the work. I felt very unsafe on this boat. I didn't want to go to sleep because I didn't know what rock we were going to hit. This skipper had hit three rocks the previous summer.

Oh, there are lots of reasons for leaving fishing. Another reason, my hands are trashed. I wake up with numb arms even when I'm not fishing. It's more of a nerve damage. My pinky and the next finger go numb. Sometimes if I sleep on my hand wrong, the whole arm goes numb. I don't need to do anything more to it.

There's no career for a lifetime in fishing for me unless I got a setnet permit, which I did think about for awhile. I thought about buying a boat, but I get too seasick, it's too big of a financial risk. And then trying to find two guys that would want to work for me. I didn't want all the headaches with mechanical breakdowns. I could handle a skiff and an outboard. And also what's happened with the price of salmon has scared me away. I want something very stable that I can do for a living.

There's a woman I know in nursing school who used to fish southeast. She had a troller, fished halibut. She's thinking about a setnet site too. We get together at school and talk fish and I think, "Oh god! What are we doing here?" When I'm over there inside a building all day, I'm thinking, "God, I wish I could go fishing!" I get back here on the water in the rain, the wind, I'm like, "Eewww!" And I'm getting older. I used to not notice the rain so much, but now I'm just getting lazy, I guess.

In the last ten years I see a lot of change in myself. Maturity, stable, balanced. Less energy. God, I had so much energy. I used to love it, just, whee! I was out west once and I remember being back up on the shelter deck and this boat was just going up and down and the spray was hitting me—I thought that was the best, exciting.

Last week I was in Henry's Bar. This other woman I know came up to me. She had just gotten off a drag trip. She appeared so hardened, so tough. Her clothes, her manner, every muscle looked tense in her. She kept looking around the bar, couldn't relax. She seemed really tense and tough. I was thinking how I used to be that way. But I don't want to be that way all the time anymore. I was like that, definitely. You had to be when you're walking the docks looking for jobs. And seeing her, I had a negative reaction: "God! Mellow out!"

They say women lose their femininity when they fish, and I think it's definitely true. There's no fault to the women. They have to put up with the ocean for one thing, to put up with the men for another. The ocean tosses you around. Get this jar, put four people in there, shake it up for about four months, that's what salmon fishing is like. I really feel like I've escaped that now.

There was one boat I tried to get on for many years. When the skipper was running it for halibut, he wanted to hire me but he couldn't because his wife was jealous and the owner's wife was jealous. I was very bummed because they made $12,000 that opening. But things have turned different now. I got on that boat and last year I was asked to tender on it. I was really shocked because they didn't want me on it years ago and now I'm going to be tendering all summer with their husbands? I was just amazed in the turnaround and I thought, "This is cool!" I couldn't be on that boat and all of a sudden I'm tendering and I'm being treated very well. I guess getting to know me changed the wives' attitudes. I met the wives and feel like I'm friends with both of them now. I think it was just the fear of some woman being on their boat. But they could see that I was just there to make some money. I wasn't there for any hanky panky. I didn't want their husbands.

It feels good to be leaving my main fishing career in this manner. I feel like I've made a change, a positive change. I'm just real happy for this job I've got now. All I have to do is pick up the phone now and say, "Hey, can I come back?" No more walking the docks and having to sell myself. I love tendering. Years ago I thought tendering was boring. Sitting in a bay all day instead of fishing. Now I've had it to here with fishing! But I'm not so sure five years from now I won't be fishing.

Afterword

When I first started this project, I considered how to reach the many women whose stories I wanted to hear. I had seen calls for submissions in Poets and Writers *for an anthology on women in sports fishing. The book* Hard-Hatted Women *was compiled the same way. I briefly considered following suit, making this public and advertising in the local paper and other papers statewide for women who fished commercially to contact me and tell their stories. But I didn't. It didn't sit right. There was something too public, too out-of-keeping with the subject. Women do not operate in fishing this way: make a public announcement, a giant splash, let everyone know they are looking for work, and then expect to be hired. And once they are, rarely do they expect any special privilege or particular attention. Women understand the rules about fishing perhaps better than men. They need to—there are more rules for women than men. And they know that if you want work, you quietly fit in. You get hired to paint a boat and then you learn how to mend net and then you calmly make yourself indispensable so that when the next crewman is injured or quits, maybe you will be hired.*

This is the way I have written and laced this book together, unobtrusively, unpresumptively, following the rules of staying quiet until you have earned a place. Though I was asked for interviews on radio and in newspapers, I declined until the process of writing was nearly complete. Aside from the more than twenty women I interviewed and their circles of friends, relatively few know of my work. And I didn't want to talk about it, not knowing if the book would find an audience, only knowing it deserved one.

Recently someone asked if the process of writing this book has changed me. My first response was a shrug of the shoulders and an "I don't think so." After all, I ended up close to where I had started. I began with the conviction that there were stories and lives to be heard and I ended with the conviction only strengthened. Along the way, however, I was persuaded to include myself, to tell my own story.

Before this I had seldom spoken of fishing to anyone outside Alaska. Those first three years fishing my husband and I were students at a conservative religious college in the Midwest. I wore dresses and heels all winter, hauled nothing heavier than books, while summers I wore rain gear and fish slime and routinely packed seventy-pound boxes up the beach in hip boots. I said nothing back in Ohio.

Several years later, in graduate school in Oregon, I picked up a small lectern, held it over my head, and moved it to another table as I prepared to give a presentation. The professor fussed and rushed to my aid, chiding me for carrying something so heavy. I looked at him, puzzled, thinking, "You've got to be kidding." If he had looked, he would have seen my arms ripple. And then I remembered—he didn't know. In a poetry workshop the next year I brought in a poem about an especially large halibut we had caught that summer. I was promptly accused by one of the women in the class of ripping off Elizabeth Bishop's poem "The Fish." I never defended myself and explained that every word was true.

Because I knew women far more committed to fishing than I was, women who loved it and chose it, women who were tougher and stronger, I always felt illegitimate. I could not call myself a fisherman to anyone, even those Outside. No one there knew about my other self, my other life. The worlds were so distant, it seemed hopeless to try to bridge them. There were times, though, when these two worlds connected. Occasionally close friends from my other life would venture all the way out to our island for a visit. One year a friend from graduate school came. Though wary of the water and philosophically opposed to killing any living creature, she stoically agreed to go out fishing one morning with Duncan and me. In the layers of rain gear, warm clothing, and boots, she was instantly transformed from a law student into one of us. I remember the sense of expectation and delight I had in her donning of my other self. By the time we got out on the water, later than usual, the morning's calm had deteriorated into a southeaster, blowing thirty perhaps—a stiff wind, but of no real concern. The skiff rode the waves expertly; Duncan drove with confidence; all was well. As we rounded the island and headed for a distant net, the wind angled across us and swept the crest of the waves into a horizontal slap across our fac-

es. Duncan and I laughed at our morning's wake-up alarm and instinctively turned our faces and backs away from the onslaught and plowed on toward the net; it was a typical morning.

Maria, though, was not faring well. The first blast caught her full in the face. I saw her gasp, cling to the sides of the skiff shaking her head to clear the saltwater from her eyes. Another wave hit and I saw her struggling for control. She was scared but was either courageous enough to keep silent and stick it out or had already figured out what you do and do not say in the skiff. After a few more drenchings I asked her, shouting over the wind, if she wanted to go back in. She nodded her wet head in defeat and apology. I remember feeling disappointed and surprised. To tell it true, I also felt solicitous toward Maria and, yes, superior. I really did believe in being tough, after all, and I prided myself on it as much as the men did. And I realized then how foreign this world was to my peers in my other life yet how familiar it was to me.

Maria's visit, and the comings of a few other friends, revealed to me my own immersion in the world of fishing. And yet, when I returned to the other world, even to academia, where I could claim "fisherman" with impunity and without fear of comparison, I still felt illegitimate and kept silent. It wasn't until years later that I could articulate why. Even without other fisherman around me I was still measuring myself against the only standard I knew—my husband and his family. All three brothers began as small children, working like men at an early age. One brother had published a textbook on our type of fishing. This family fishing operation was one of the most established in the area. They were expert; they were in it heart, soul, and body. I was a novice, already learning to choose self-preservation. Because of our isolation on a remote island, I knew no lesser commitment to fishing than theirs. Now I recognize the women and men who fish only six weeks a year in Bristol Bay or who work two-day-a-week openings in Prince William Sound who wear this label. There is a whole range of commitments and work ethics and degrees of expertise, I have found. We each name ourselves as we want to be known.

There was still more to the silence issue, though, more than the gap between the two worlds, more than falling short of a perceived standard. It had to do with fishing itself, the way fishermen talk, what you do and do not talk about. There was a whole set of rules I had silently absorbed and just as silently lived by. I, the one who loved to socialize and philoso-

phize and analyze, knew implicitly where the boundaries were and fol-
lowed them. You didn't talk about how hard something was, how bad you
felt, that you were scared in that last storm, that you were ready for the
fish to stop filling the net, that there might be an easier way of putting out
the nets, that the weather was too rough, that maybe righting the corks in
the outgoing tide was a waste of time, that your fingers were too numb to
mend the web . . . All this is irrelevant to the work that must be done. It
may be your entire reality at the moment, but you keep working, say noth-
ing. Outside of your own fishing operation, out of the skiff, off the boat,
there are more rules. You don't say how many fish you caught, where you
caught them, how you're doing compared to last year, that your expenses
are killing you . . . And so I didn't talk about fishing at all, I only lived it.

Only now, after the interviewing and transcribing and writing and think-
ing of these last three years, have I begun to open that life up and to link
sometimes competing worlds: commercial fishing and academia; privacy
and exploration; stoicism and articulation. It has been done quietly, pri-
vately, but something has happened in the midst of it all. During the in-
terviews with each woman, as we sat over coffee with the tape player run-
ning, there were many moments when we erupted into laughter over a
shared experience. There were flashes of recognition and incredulity—"You
too?!" Though my fishing experience was limited to a single fishery, I saw
through their experiences and lives, my own. The cloak, this one made of
polyurethane rain gear, fell off. The secrets were out. The world did not
rock or even tilt, however. As revelatory as it has been for me, the revela-
tions, too, have been private and quiet: just knowing that my own concerns
and passages and traumas fit a larger pattern, a pattern shared by other
women, has given me perspective. It's a perspective that moves in two di-
rections, into the heart of the deeply personal and then out again, beyond,
into the web and network of other lives and experiences that enlarge my
own. There is great comfort in knowing I am a small part of something
much larger. I treasure this.

Along the way, too, I realized that though I had sectioned and arranged
these stories by issues, this book was really more than that. "Issues" car-
ries on its back the weight of academia, of the intellectual and the imper-
sonal. As I began to add my own story to the others, though reluctantly at
first, I began to see how much this book traced my past and, strangely, how
it may map my future.

Because although the book itself is completed the "issues" here are not resolved; really, they are only beginning. My four children, the third generation to fish here, catapult this topic from casual intellectual interest to deep personal concern. I worry about many things already revealed in these chapters. I have seen enough family casualties that I cannot ignore the risks. How do we balance a work ethic and the inflexible demands of fishing with nurturance, providing the love and protection a child of any age needs? In an occupation that demands endurance and strong backs, what if my daughter or son has neither? In the frenzied four-month harvest of fish, where clocks are irrelevant to the job, how long do they work, how much should they play? How do we allow for differences in strength, in motivation, in skill in a business that makes no such distinctions? And the hardest question of all: What if my husband and I do not agree on the answers?

And what about their feelings—Will the children accept the balance of gains and losses, that though they will never play in Little League, go on vacations, or spend the summer at camp, they will gain courage, self-confidence, a life on the water in a world stunning in its beauty and purity? What if the familiarity of this life holds them so tightly that even as adults they foreclose other professions just to return to fish? I have seen both sides of all these scenarios. Ultimately, for me this book is not about issues: it is about the hopes, the integrity of our family, all six of us, and our larger extended family of fifteen. It has to do with the rest of my life, with my children's' lives. The force of this occupation and lifestyle will shape their future, not just what they will do, but who they will be as people.

Some women reading this will detect my near fade to invisibility here, the movement from a concentration on my individual struggles to concern over my children's', as I ponder the future. This may sound like the same old story of femininity and tradition—the loss of the self to one's family, the defining of the self through roles. Perhaps this movement will seem startling coming from someone involved in a lifestyle and an occupation far from traditional for a woman. This part of my story surely is wrapped up in "traditional feminine" concerns—and other women who fish and have children share them—but it just as surely is about me. The hardest part of my journey is over. The process that began for me eighteen years ago has brought me, finally, to a place where I can live and prosper. Finding my place in a new world, learning to handle the risks of injury and drowning, surviving without amputating emotions and relationships, bal-

ancing the need for acceptance within the family with the need for change—all of this has been slowly, painfully accomplished. The outcome was never sure, though, and the progress was never steady. At several points along the way, I was nearly consumed. This past I know; the rest I do not. As I look at my children I see that they must travel this same perilous way, but they journey as children, not as young adults. I feel so keenly their innocence, their vulnerability. They are young—so much remains to be lived and done and cried and fought and hugged over on our island, in our skiff, in the midst of the fish. And there is no escape, nor would I want there to be, from my place in the center of all that.

But there's more. This dynamic of dependence and interdependence is not limited to maternal relationships or traditional femininity. The same interplay is at work among our crew, among the brothers who run our operation, among the entire fishing operation. We lay our positions, our professions, our identities down on the beach as we come ashore that first day of the season. Biblical scholar, musician, writer, student, attorney, teacher, rancher—we give up our individual selves to live corporately, communally. To think about my future individually in relation to fishing is foreign to all that we do and who we are for those four months. Though I have moved to another island, though I insist on some degree of individuality and control over that life, I find that, finally, I choose to belong to the world that is larger than myself.

And yet, and yet, it is not simple or easy. Part of my slow growth has been to find the way to live within this "commune" but find a way out of it as well to a larger community. I remember the fourth or fifth season when I was still struggling with disillusionment, though privately. Part of me felt betrayed by the demands of the work and what it stole from my marriage, but I could not speak about it. There seemed so little choice in those days. At the annual Fourth of July picnic, the one event that gathered all the fishermen and fishing families in the bay, I remember looking around the group of sixty or so. They were all dressed as I was, in moss-green Helly Hansen rain gear—it was drizzling, of course. In clumps of four and five, they were talking earnestly, some laughing. I felt guilty that I did not love fishing as everyone else seemed to. I joined a group of women, a rare treat, but we talked then of fishing, the same things the men spoke of. What would happen to the prices? Was there going to be a strike? Why hadn't the sock- eye run come through as strong in June as expected? There was no con-

scious strategizing, but I knew that if this was going to be my world I wanted to live inside of it rather than outside: the quickest way out the door was to complain and break loyalties. Eight years later I found myself talking with a friend not about fish prices or strikes but about our families, our feelings, our struggles with the isolation, the schedules, the work. I saw her for the first time as someone not Herculean but vulnerable, even emotionally exhausted. I had no idea. Our friendship flourished, though we saw one another perhaps three times in a season. And there were other women, other visits and walks where we talked first about fishing, then found the way to talk deeply about what we cared about most.

I remember the amazement and relief I felt when these walls came down. It took me a long time to identify what had been missing in my life before then because I thought I already had it. In the extended family I married into I had found some deep and satisfying relationships right next door— our houses were just feet apart. Ten years later, when my husband and I moved to our own island with our own beginning family, I was lonely at first but came increasingly to appreciate the isolation: it unified us, shaped us into a common identity. Our lives in the winter seemed a constant struggle against entropy—each of us, no matter how young, moving in ever-expanding circles away from the family center. But there, on our island, for three or four months, we inhabited the exact same space. I counted this a blessing, this time with my children and the intensity of relationship and understanding that resulted, but it was not enough; it became another kind of isolation. It is part of the irony of the wilderness and of commercial fishing. We are attracted to it because of the independence it allows, yet we find ourselves compressed into places and relationships of great dependence, and often beyond our choosing. This is especially true for fishing families who share their food, their skiffs, their bunks, and their own small cabins with hired crew.

Other women feel the compression and isolation too. I know, not always by what we reveal to one another, but by the intensity of frustration we feel when fishing schedules keep us apart, by the joy if and when we actually meet. Now, with these other friends, even while out on the fishing grounds, we seldom speak of salmon and prices. We save that for public conversation. And though it is commercial fishing that has brought us together, and though all our lives are enmeshed in it, we are building community around and above it, even in spite of it.

This returns me to the earlier question, "Has writing this book changed me?" My answer now is "yes." I know that I am part of a fishing tradition, that others share my experiences. I have found and continue to find ways to bridge the various worlds I inhabit, and I look forward to helping my children find their own ways in and out of these worlds. And in writing this book, in speaking what is known but seldom given voice within fishing families and especially among them, is to make all of us fishermen part of a new tradition, one that moves us beyond our own insular worlds into true community.

I do not know how others will judge the lives and words in this book. It does matter: I live here. This is my community, my family, my friends, my life. I am thoroughly entangled in the net. It is because of this rather than in spite of it that I have dared to ask, question, and write. And finally, now, this web of stories has been released to catch what it may.

Notes on the Fishers

Virginia Adams began her Alaskan fishing career in Kodiak, where she got her first job seining for salmon. She soon was working year round, gillnetting for cod and trawling for cod and pollock until the birth of her son, Gabe, seven years ago. While her husband Jonathan continues a year-round fishing schedule, Virginia works a half-year season, fishing herring in the spring and setnetting for salmon summer and fall at her setnet site in Uganik Bay on Kodiak Island. When not fishing, she is active in fisheries politics. For her narratives see pp. 15–17 and 54–58.

Holly Berry fished king crab in the Bering Sea during the boom years of the seventies and early eighties. During that time the stocks of king crab, the most prized species, suddenly and inexplicably exploded. Simultaneously, the demand for crab increased just as explosively. At the height of the boom, when the crab sold for more than $5 a pound and boats fished several hundred pots, the boat owner and even the crew could become rich in a single two-month season. On a highliner crab boat, a crew member could take home $50,000–$100,000 for those two months. Holly retired from crabbing in 1983 after an injury. She lives in Kodiak, where she runs Holly's Gear Service, building and repairing crab pots. For her narratives, see pp. 24–27 and 110–14.

Sandy Earle has been involved in salmon fishing for twenty-five years. She and her husband, Danny, began fishing for Dora Aga in Larsen Bay. Later they bought two salmon setnet permits of their own. Sandy and Danny spend winters in Seattle and work spring, summer, and fall at their fish camp on the west side of Kodiak Island. Kodiak's salmon season is one of the longest in the state, beginning early in June and extending through September. For her narrative, see pp. 130–34.

Leslie Leyland Fields lives in Kodiak, Alaska, with her husband and four children. Every summer she moves with her family to a small island one hun-

dred miles from Kodiak to work in a family-owned commercial fishing operation. Winters she teaches English at the University of Alaska at Kodiak. She
has master of arts degrees in journalism and English and a master of fine arts
degree in creative nonfiction. Her first book about fishing was a volume of
poetry entitled *The Water under Fish.*

Cinda Gilmer began her fishing career salmon seining. After a few seasons
around Kodiak Island and the Alaska Peninsula, she moved out to the Aleutians, where she fished halibut around Sand Point and then drift gillnetted
for salmon in False Pass. Today Cinda, her husband, Tyler, and their five children live in Florida. She writes, "I'm not fishing for fish anymore; I'm involved
in community Bible study and am 'fishing for men and women' as it says in
Matthew 4:19." For her narratives, see pp. 19–24 and 91–96.

Christine Holmes lived in Cordova, Alaska, and worked year round for more
than a decade in a number of Alaska's fisheries, including pollock, herring,
salmon, and cod. After her diagnosis of breast cancer, Christine continued
to fish, primarily in Prince William Sound, until shortly before her death in
the spring of 1996. The many friends she left behind speak of Christine's pas-
sion for life, her constant energy, and her love for commercial fishing. For her
narratives, see pp. 62–67 and 105–10.

Mary Jacobs has owned and skippered a fishing vessel for more than twenty
years, fishing halibut, herring, and salmon on the Alaska Peninsula and around
Kodiak Island. This next salmon season, she will again have an all-female crew
with the additions of her daughter Imy, age eight, and her college-age daughter, Balika. The salmon runs around Kodiak Island are thriving, as are many of
the salmon runs in Alaska. The abundance of salmon, however, has led to sharp-
ly declining prices in recent years. Pink salmon, once worth $.55 a pound, have
recently been selling for $.10 a pound. For her narrative, see pp. 75–80.

Lisa Jakubowski has worked as a commercial fisherman for twelve years in
various fisheries, including longlining for cod and halibut and seining and
setnetting for salmon. She recently completed nurse's training and is now a
registered nurse living in Bend, Oregon. She writes, "I really miss the fun part
of fishing, but I'm tired of putting up with all the other stuff that goes with
it. I'm finally out of fishing for good." For her narratives, see pp. 58–62 and
140–44.

Lori Francisco Johanson and *Terri Francisco Barber* grew up in a fishing
family and have setnetted for salmon off Kodiak Island all their lives. Though

married and living Outside, each with three preschool children, they find it increasingly difficult to return to fish with their parents and siblings. Each year they return they are sure it is their last. Because salmon setnetting is more shore based than other fisheries, it is common for extended families, even with young children, to live and work together. For their narrative, see pp. 134–40.

Laurie Jolly and *Rebecque Raigoza* beach seine for salmon around Kodiak Island. Beach seining is, by definition, more labor intensive and nomadic than most other gear types. Beach seine fishers on Kodiak Island cannot by law erect a cabin. Thus in addition to moving from place to place in search of fish by day, Laurie and Rebecque would camp out at night on remote beaches where they were prey to rain, frequent windstorms, and occasional bears. After two intensive seasons, Laurie returned to California, where she now works for a corporate real estate firm. Rebecque fished one more season and has since returned to graduate school. For their narratives, see pp. 45–51 and 127–30.

Laurie Knapp began commercial fishing in Alaska when she was seventeen and soon found herself part of the "crab fever" that infected the fleet in the seventies and early eighties. Based out of Dutch Harbor, she witnessed the violence, the drugs, the recklessness fueled by the flush of fast money. When the crab declined, Laurie went on to work in other fisheries until the birth of her two daughters. Today she lives in Kodiak, works construction, and continues to fish salmon. This last season she crewed for Mary Jacobs. For her narrative, see pp. 67–71.

Sylvia Lange, an Alaskan native, grew up fishing with her father, mother, and sister out of Cordova. Beginning in her late teens, she skippered her own vessel for a number of years, working the Copper River Flats area, famed for its sandbars, violent waves, and turbulent tide changes. Now, along with her husband and three children, she buys and processes fish as the owner of a cannery in Cordova. For her narrative, see pp. 17–19.

Debra Nielsen began her career on the water salvaging and rebuilding sunken boats. She soon moved into commercial fishing off Kodiak Island and the Alaska Peninsula, eventually running her own salmon seining boat and crew. In 1987 she was one of two survivors in the sinking of the *Wayward Wind*. Since that event, she has turned to other pursuits: running an import gift shop, working with her husband, Mark, a commercial fisherman, and raising their daughter, Danica. For her narratives, see pp. 85–91 and 120–24.

Theresa Peterson has worked nearly ten years longlining for cod and halibut and seining for salmon and herring. Theresa has excelled at setting the skates and picking the gear at a fast and often dangerous pace. She lives in Kodiak with her husband, also a commercial fisherman, and alternates her time at sea with her husband's so they can share in the raising of their two children. For her narratives, see pp. 30–33 and 100–105.

Leslie Smith, based on Kodiak Island, skippered a salmon seining boat for three years before switching to salmon setnetting. She now owns and runs her own setnetting operation. Because the nets are attached to shore and are stationary, with no need to pursue or search for fish, this fishery can be easier on fishing families. Each summer Leslie brings her two preschool daughters with her to her isolated fish camp on the Shelikof Strait. Though constantly battling rough weather, she is grateful she can merge work and mothering. For her narratives, see pp. 34–39 and 80–85.

Peggy Smith worked on crab boats in the Bering Sea from 1976 to 1987, one of only a handful of women in a fleet of over two hundred boats. She started out as cook, then maneuvered a position as deckhand, one of the first women to do so. In that position, she witnessed the precipitous rise and fall of the king crab. The fishery peaked in 1980, when 29 million pounds of crab were brought to market. By 1982, only 3 million crab were harvested. In 1983, the king crab season closed. Peggy lives in Kodiak with her husband and two children and drives trucks for a living. For her narrative, see pp. 114–20.

Martha Sutro has returned to teaching high school English after a 1990–93 hiatus of crab fishing in the Bering Sea. While king crab stocks are still marginal, other species of crab, such as opilio and tanner, have remained stable, though they are declining as well. Martha lives in Mill Valley, California, and says her life is relatively normal, though she is "homesick for the physical world" she encountered in Alaska. For her narrative, see pp. 39–44.